A–Z of Leeds

Places - People - History

Paul Chrystal

Acknowledgements

Without the generous help from the people of Leeds this book would be considerably less informative and significantly less colourful. I would therefore like to thank the following for their assistance in the provision of information and for some stunning photography: Anys Williams at Anita Morris Associates for the Corn Exchange images; Susan Williamson at Temple Works; Sally Hughes, Assistant Librarian Manager, Local and Family History Library, Leeds Central Library for the Leodis images; Peter Higginbotham, workhouses.org.uk; Ollie Jenkins, Picture House Administrator, Hyde Park Picture House; and Andrew Bannister, Head of Media Relations, Leeds Teaching Hospitals NHS Trust.

First published 2019

Amberley Publishing
The Hill, Stroud, Gloucestershire, GL5 4EP
www.amberley-books.com

ISBN 978 1 4456 8913 5 (print)
ISBN 978 1 4456 8914 2 (ebook)

British Library Cataloguing in Publication Data.
A catalogue record for this book is available from the British Library.

Typesetting by Aura Technology and Software Services, India. Printed in Great Britain.

Contents

Introduction

Leeds is a city of great history and heritage. From its beginnings as a religious and agricultural centre in the Middle Ages to its twenty-first-century status as one of the UK's leading digital and information technology hubs, it has always been one of the cities at the forefront of progress in the UK.

This book is a manageable and convenient survey of the city's history, which can be read sequentially from A to Z or dipped into at leisure, informing and entertaining visitor and resident alike. By ranging through the alphabet it covers aspects of Leeds past and present, describing famous Leeds people – writers, war heroes, fighters for women's rights and villains – some of the city's stunning architecture and its rich and varied culture.

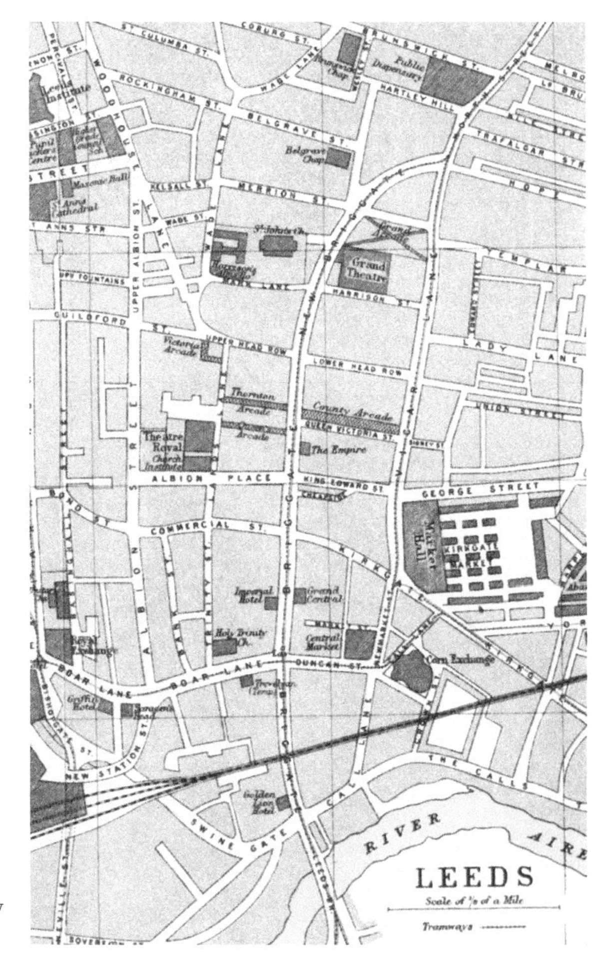

A map of central Leeds published by Bartholomew of Edinburgh in 1909.

Armley Mills (1788), Canal Road

Armley Mills and its history reflects the history of the textile industry in Leeds. That long history begins in the mid-sixteenth century when local clothier Richard Booth leased 'Armley Millnes' from Henry Saville. We hear from a 1707 document: 'That Fulling Mill in Armley ... containing two wheels and four stocks ... also the water corn mill and all the fulling mills ... containing one wheel and two stocks.' By 1788 Armley could boast five waterwheels powering eighteen fulling stocks.

Armley Mills today – a superb museum.

The 1904 Platt-built condenser mule (self-acting) at Armley Mills Industrial Museum, which was used for spinning wool.

Fulling is one of the end processes in cloth production. It involves pounding the cloth with big hammers in pits filled with water, urine and 'fullers earth', making the fibres mat together or 'felt'. You can still see fulling hammers in the mill today. The necessary urine, a source of ammonia, was collected from nearby families, who saved it up especially for that purpose.

In 1788 Armley Mills was bought by Colonel Thomas Lloyd, a wealthy Leeds cloth merchant who made it the world's largest woollen mill. In 1804 Benjamin Gott bought the mills. In November 1805 disaster struck when the mill was almost entirely gutted by fire. Gott rebuilt it from fireproof materials, using brick and iron wherever possible. The early mills were considerable fire hazards, with airborne fibres igniting and setting fire to flammable structures. The 1788 the mill had been powered by five waterwheels while the 1805 mill was engined by two metal wheels, which went by the names of 'Wellington' and 'Blucher', allied heroes in the Napoleonic Wars. They were rated at 70 horsepower. It is Gott's mill that you can see at the museum today.

Armley Mills went from strength to strength with export markets in North and South America, Europe and the Far East. In 1805 the mill was the world's largest woollen mill containing eighteen fulling stocks and fifty looms. Gott was one of

Britain's largest employers in Britain. After his death in 1840 his sons John and William introduced the first steam engine to Armley Mills in 1850 to supplement the waterwheels, which continued operating into the 1860s.

In 1971 the mill closed and was bought by Leeds City Council, reopening in 1982 as Leeds Industrial Museum. Botany Bay Yard is close by – so named because it was the first place in England where wool from Botany Bay in Australia was landed. The museum has collections of textile machinery, railway equipment and heavy engineering.

Armley Gaol

HMP Leeds is a Category B men's prison, which opened in 1847 and is still referred to locally as 'Armley Gaol'. The suitably grim-looking building, disturbingly visible for miles around, was built with four wings radiating from a central point, each of which had three landings of cells – on the 'then modern penitentiary principal with four radial wings'. It was responsible for incarcerating prisoners sentenced in the West Riding, but also took over the gruesome task from York Castle of executing West Riding prisoners. Ninety-three men and one woman suffered the death penalty at Armley between 1864 and 1961 – an average of almost one every year. Hungarian Zsiga Pankotia was the last to swing, courtesy of Harry Allen, in 1961 for the murder of Jack Eli Myers in a house burglary in Roundhay.

The last double execution at Armley Gaol was that of Thomas Riley and John Roberts on 29 April 1932. They were hanged by Tom Pierrepoint. It took ninety seconds to complete. Riley was hanged for the murder of fifty-two-year-old Elizabeth Castle with whom he was cohabiting. Roberts was executed for the murder of greengrocer Alfred Gill, whom he had battered to death. Double executions stopped in 1954 and were outlawed by the 1957 Homicide Act. The extra time they took subjected the prisoners to unnecessary and avoidable anxiety and suffering.

Arthur Osborne had the misfortune to be hanged on his birthday at Armley. Osborne was found guilty of the murder of seventy-year-old Ernest Westwood on 25 September 1948. He had stabbed and robbed him in his home. Osborne then fled to Chichester with a view to marrying Dorothy Ball even though he was already married – his wife was in a psychiatric hospital. At the end of his three-day trial at Leeds Assizes the jury recommended mercy, but the Home Secretary disagreed and Osborne was duly hanged on his twenty-eight birthday, 30 December 1948. The last execution on the old A wing was that of nineteen-year-old Walter Sharpe on 30 March 1950. Sharpe was hanged for the robbery and murder of jeweller Abraham Harry Levine in November 1949.

Two new wings were added in 1994, while a new gate complex opened in September 2002. The prison can accommodate up to 1,212 prisoners in 551 regular cells and in six residential units, a segregation unit, First Night Centre, Vulnerable Prisoner Unit and inpatients' Healthcare Facility.

Botched executions were not uncommon at this time. In the early days and 'a shocking scene' was reported by the *Yorkshire Post* newspaper following the hanging of thirty-seven-year-old John Henry Johnson on Wednesday 3 April 1877. Johnson had been condemned for the murder of Amos Waite, who had been showing interest in Johnson's wife, Amelia, on Boxing Day 1876. After a drunken quarrel in the pub where they were all drinking, Johnson went home, returning a little while later with a gun to shoot Waite in the chest. Thomas Askern was called to Leeds to dispatch Johnson and had made the usual preparations on the Tuesday afternoon, but when he pulled the lever the rope broke and Johnson plummeted through the trap. He was immediately rescued by the warders, who removed his straps and hood and sat him on a chair. It took Askern ten minutes to rig a new rope and reset the trap before Johnson could again be led up onto it. This time the rope held but it was reported that Johnson 'died hard', struggling for some four minutes on the rope. His death was formally recorded as being from asphyxia, but no official mention was made of the failure of first attempt to hang him. It was to be Askern's last execution at Armley.

The grim and bleak Armley Gaol. (Courtesy of www.capitalpunishmentuk.org/armley.html)

Barnbow Munitions Factory – National Filling Factory No. 1

Barnbow, a city within a city, was a First World War munitions factory located between Cross Gates and Garforth, officially known as National Filling Factory No. 1. Despite the prodigious and dangerous work that was done to assist the war effort at Barnbow, Barnbow is, sadly, best known for the massive explosion that killed thirty-five of the women workers in 1916.

When war was declared, shells were being filled and armed at Leeds Forge Company, Armley, which by August 1915 was filling 10,000 shells every week. This, however, was insufficient to meet demand, so the newly formed and enterprising Leeds Munitions Committee introduced production of shells at Hunslet and Newlay (Horsforth). A site was selected at Barnbow between Crossgates and Garforth, and railway tracks were laid, running into the factory complex to carry materials in and finished goods out. There were 13 miles of wide-gauge railway track and 10 miles of narrow trolley track. Platforms over 800 feet long were added to the nearby railway station to help transport workers to and from work at the site. The Yorkshire Power Company erected a 10-kv

Barnbow girls making box lids for cartridge packing cases out of empty propellant boxes. They are using circular saws (without protective guards) to cut the wood to size to make the box lids. (Courtesy of Leodis. © Leeds Library & Information Services)

Filling shells at Newlay.

overhead line to a sub-station and this, in conjunction with a boiler house and heating plant, provided power for the heating and lighting of the entire complex. The electric power cables extended for over 28 miles. A water main was laid to deliver 200,000 gallons of water per day and a 90,000-gallon collecting and screening tank was built to collect waste, which was pumped to the Leeds Sewerage Works at Killingbeck.

The service mains – water, sewage and fire – extended for 33 miles, and the steam and hot-water piping for 60 miles. Coal was supplied by rail from Garforth Collieries Ltd and Wheldale Coal Co. In April 1916, the first batch of thirty 4.5-inch shells were filled, with the output quickly increasing to 6,000 shells a day when the number of shifts was increased from two to three.

Recruitment took place at an employment bureau at Wellesley Barracks, Leeds. The first batch of employees was sent to Woolwich for one month's training, after which training was all done at Barnbow. Around 130,000 female applicants were interviewed. One-third of the staff was from Leeds while others commuted from York, Castleford, Selby, Tadcaster, Wetherby, Knaresborough, Wakefield and Harrogate. By October 1916 the workforce exceeded 16,000 people, 93 per cent of whom were women and girls – 'the Barnbow Lasses'. Thirty-eight trains per day, 'Barnbow Specials', carried the workers to and from work.

The women worked a system of three eight-hour shifts: 6 a.m. to 2 p.m., 2 p.m. to 10 p.m. and 10 p.m. to 6 a.m. usually on a six-days-a-week rota, with Saturday off every three weeks – there were no holidays. A typical munition worker's earnings for a full week averaged £3; the girls who swept up the waste for recycling earned £1 17*s* a week. Extra money was paid to workers in the dangerous-powder room. At one point the weekly wage bill totalled £24,000.

Shells were also filled by the Leeds Forge Company at Armley.

Barnbow workers – women and men.

The information board at the site of the factory.

Barnbow lasses.

The Barnbow Disaster

Barnbow was, and is, Leeds's worst disaster in terms of fatalities: thirty-five women were killed. Some aspects of health and safety at Barnbow were reassuringly advanced. Sandbags and protective shields were all around the place; sprinklers and drenchers were attached to the magazines; and there were fireproof doors and protective earthworks. There was good ventilation in the work areas, especially in the Amatol factories. Initially staff were limited to a fortnight stretch anywhere TNT was handled. All workers had to pass a medical examination before starting their employment; those working in dangerous-area zones had a periodic medical examination. A female superintendent, supported by a staff of welfare workers, was appointed to make regular visits to employees, either during work or at meal times. They also visited anyone off sick or absent from work for any length of time.

Tennis courts were provided. The site fire brigade was an early introduction. Initially it was all men, but later girls were trained up. Eventually, thirty girls and six firemen, under the command of an experienced London firemaster, made up the brigade. Units of the Royal Defence Corps provided security, maintaining a twenty-four-hour patrol of the security fence and gates. The superintendent of police and three inspectors controlled the male police, while a female superintendent was in charge of policewomen for female search purposes. All personnel were required to wear identity discs and carry permits; there were frequent body and bag searches. Dangerous areas were under constant surveillance, with 'safe' areas reserved for smokers. There was a complete press blackout of the area.

Despite this the work was still very dangerous. Workers who handled the explosives stripped to their underwear and wore smocks, puttees, caps, rubber gloves and rubber-soled boots to avoid sparks. Cigarettes and matches were obviously banned, as were combs and hairpins to prevent static electricity. Workers were allowed to drink as much barley water and milk as they liked and, to help with the milk, Barnbow had its own farm, with a herd of 120 cows producing 300 gallons of milk per day. Working with cordite turns the skin yellow, and the only known antidote was milk. Because of the yellowness of the women's skin, they were called 'the Barnbow Canaries'.

Fire drill at Barnbow.

On Tuesday 5 December 1916, 170 women and girls had just started their night shift in one of the fusing rooms – 4.5-inch shells were being filled, fused and packed in Room 42. At 10.27 p.m. there was a massive explosion, which killed thirty-five women outright and maimed and injured many more. Many of the dead were only identifiable by their identity discs. The injured were taken to Leeds General Infirmary with the help of the factory medical staff, the ambulance corps and the voluntary motor transport section. Production was interrupted only for a short time, and once the bodies were recovered, other girls immediately volunteered to replace them in Room 42.

For reasons of security, none of this was made public until 1924. At the time death notices appeared in the *Yorkshire Evening Post*, simply stating cause of death as 'killed by accident' and other euphemisms. There were two further explosions at the factory: the first in March 1917, killing two girls; the other in May 1918, killing three men.

Barnbow was Britain's premier shell factory between 1914 and 1918. By 11 November 1918, a total of 566,000 tons of ammunition had been shipped to the various fronts; over 36 million breech-loading cartridges had been produced; 24.75 million shells had been filled; and a further 19.25 million shells had been fused and packed – a grand total of 566,000 tons of finished ammunition exported. Of 18-pounder shells 9.25million were filled which, if laid end to end, covered a distance of 3,200 miles.

Apart from setting up the dignified memorial, in 2012 the people of Leeds named a number of parks, buildings and streets in memory of the 'Barnbow Lasses'. The names of those who died are listed in the roll of honour in Colton Methodist Church and in York Minster, near to the Five Sisters Window.

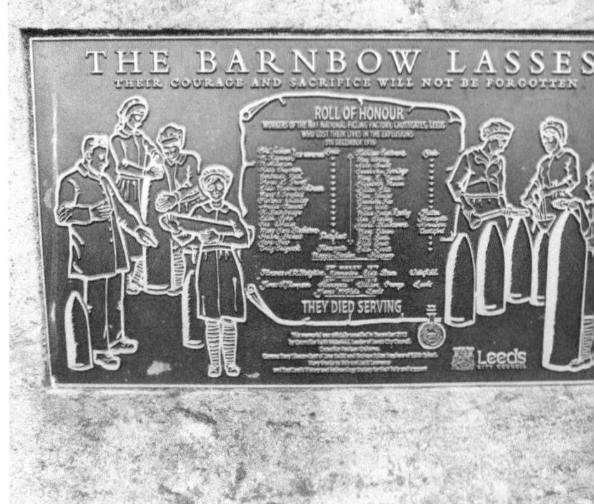

Above left: The memorial in York Minster.

Above right: The memorial at the site.

The Beeston Brotherhood

The Beeston Brotherhood was a Tolstoyan group of anarchist pacifists and vegetarians who came to settle in Leeds from Surrey in 1904. They were investigated under DORA, the Defence of the Realm Act, while their literature was deemed prejudicial to recruitment, training and discipline of the armed services. The anarchist Alf Kitson was a prominent member, who was described as a joiner when he appeared in Hull Police Court charged with refusing to fill up a registration under the Registration Act, on 21 February 1916. He asserted:

> I refuse to give you any information. I do not believe in slaying my fellow men, and I will not have part or lot in the making of munitions of war. I have no more faith in you than I have in the Kaiser. You all believe in murder and robbery, and you will not give justice to the workers of our land in times of peace. You make the wars, so fight them yourselves. I have had nothing to do with the foreign policy, never having voted for representatives in Parliament. You may do what you like, but I refuse to assist you.

He had already been summonsed under the same charge on 4 February, but had failed to appear and was arrested. The magistrate urged Kitson to change his mind, but he persisted and was heavily fined. The Leeds founder, Tom Ferris, with accomplice Overbury, was jailed in Armley where they went on hunger strike. Overbury was force-fed, but the medical authorities refused to sanction force-feeding Ferris due to his 'weak heart'. More arrests followed at known Brotherhood addresses, which became refuges for conscientious objectors.

Alan Bennett (b. 1934)

> We started off trying to set up a small anarchist community, but people wouldn't obey the rules.
>
> Alan Bennett

Alan Bennett's early days in Armley define the man, and inform much of his work. His regular forays over forty years to his house in the Dales village of Clapham further reinforce his associations with Yorkshire and add a rural landscape to the decidedly urban, working-class and back-to-back backdrop that is Armley. His uncanny ear for Yorkshire dialect, the absurd and just plain daft things people sometimes say, office gossip minutiae, and the eccentricities of the ordinary man and woman is unmatched. His mother ('Mam') is a source of some of this, with such axiomatic jewels as, on the trouble with being bald, said that 'You'd never know where to stop washing your face' – a gift that he elsewhere described as 'an unerring grasp of inessentials which is the prerogative of mothers'.

Armley is famous for two very different things: the forbidding Armley Gaol and the amiable Alan Bennett. Alan Bennett grew up in the Leeds suburb before going to Oxford in 1954. His father was a violin-playing butcher; his mother, Lilian Mary Peel, a housewife who sadly suffered from depression and Alzheimer's later in life. He attended Leeds Modern School, now Lawnswood School in Otley Road, where a plaque proudly proclaims that their library is named after him. Nothing could be more fitting, as it was the public library in Armley that provided boyhood Bennett with an early, unshakeable grounding in reading, books and an enduring and acute observation of characters – Armley-type characters – their foibles and their exquisite mundanities.

In 2011 Bennett took a small, albeit influential, step in repaying his debt to the council-run Armley Library when he spoke in support of keeping the Kensal Rise Library open – local to where he now lives in North London. Kensal Rise closed despite Alan Bennett's efforts: 'Libraries have to be local; the early part of a child's reading life is vital.' He knew that was true from personal experience, just as it was true for hundreds of other writers including, for example, Laurie Lee, who 'gorged' on Joyce and Huxley at Stroud Public Library. Bennett has famously said (in *The London Review of Books*, Vol. 33, No. 15, 28 July 2011, pp. 3–7) that, 'Having learned to read there was nothing in the house on which to practise my newly acquired skill.' And so Armley Public Library then became an obligatory weekly outing for Mr and Mrs Bennett and their two sons. An early favourite were the *Dr Dolittle* stories of Hugh Lofting and Richmal Crompton's *William* books.

One of Bennett's earliest descriptions of Leeds finds him saying, 'Like the other great Northern cities still intact in 1951, but though I was not blind to its architectural splendours, unfashionable though at that time they were, it was a soot-blackened, wholly 19th-century city' (*London Review of Books*, Vo. 36, No. 12, 19 June 2014, pp. 29–30).

Richard Hoggart's *The Uses of Literacy* (1957) had an important influence on Bennett, providing a simultaneous literary and urban landscape all of its own, which he first read in New York in 1963.

Original cast of *Beyond the Fringe*. From the left: Dudley Moore, Alan Bennett, Peter Cook and Jonathan Miller. The revue played on Broadway from 1962 to 1964. (Photographer: Friedman-Abeles, New York)

Alan Bennett is much, much more than a font of classic one-liners. Yet he is the master of pithy, much of which was honed in and mined from his early Armley life. Here are some delicious Bennett quotations:

> 'What I'm above all primarily concerned with is the substance of life, the pith of reality. If I had to sum up my work, I suppose that's it really: I'm taking the pith out of reality.' *Writing Home* (1994) diary entry for 25 July 1985, p. 144
>
> On being asked by Sir Ian McKellen in 1997 whether he was gay or straight: 'That's a bit like asking a man crawling across the Sahara whether he would prefer Perrier or Malvern water.'
>
> 'At eighty, things do not occur; they recur.' *The Uncommon Reader*, 2007
>
> 'History is just one f*cking thing after another.' *The History Boys*, 2004
>
> 'Definition of a classic: a book everyone is assumed to have read and often thinks they have.'
>
> 'Mark my words. When a society has to resort to the lavatory for its humour, the writing is on the wall.' *Forty Years On*, 1968
>
> 'It was the kind of library he had only read about in books.' *The Uncommon Reader*, 2007

The Black Prince

Edward of Woodstock (1330–76), better known as the Black Prince, was the eldest son of Edward III and Philippa of Hainault, and the father of Richard II of England. The

The Black Prince getting himself together in City Square. (Courtesy of Leodis. © Leeds Library & Information Services)

equestrian Black Prince statue in City Square took seven years to complete. It was cast in Belgium because it was too big for any British foundry. The statue was brought to City Square by barge from Hull along the Aire & Calder Navigation and unveiled on 16 September 1903.

The Black Prince himself has absolutely nothing to do with Leeds. The statue was a gift from Colonel Thomas Walter Harding, Lord Mayor of Leeds between 1898 and 1899, and was just a historical figure Harding happened to admire, symbolising as he did democracy and chivalry. The less said about his penchant for the *chevauchée* strategy (burning and pillaging towns and farms) the better.

The Bread Arch

On 5 October 1894, the citizens of Leeds built an archway made of bread to mark the visit by the Duke and Duchess of York (the future George V and Queen Mary), who were there to open the Medical School and College Hall of Yorkshire College (now Leeds University). The novel structure spanned the width of Commercial Street, near Briggate, weighed 5 tons and was made of white, brown and spiced loaves. It was the brainchild of Henry Child, who ran the Mitre Hotel, to which the arch was attached. William Morris, who

The bread arch.

ran a bakery in Pack Horse Yard, baked the bread, which was the equivalent of hundreds of loaves, the flour for which cost £20 and was paid for by Henry Child. The plan was to distribute the loaves to the poor after the visit, but rain stopped that.

Burton's

Burton's was founded by Montague Burton in Chesterfield in 1904 under the name of the Cross-Tailoring Company. Burton himself was a Russian-Jewish immigrant, originally Meshe David Osinsky. He arrived in England from Russia aged fifteen working as a peddler, and three years later borrowed £100 from a relative to open the Cross-Tailoring Company. Records show that the first purchase of ready-made suits was on 8 June 1905, from Zimmerman Bros, wholesale clothiers of Leeds. The growing business moved to Elmwood Mills, Camp Road in Leeds, but by 1914 it had outgrown these premises and transferred to Concord Mills, Concord Street.

By 1914 the number of Burton shops increased to fourteen and their made-to-measure service was well on the way to becoming the largest in the world. The First World War saw Burton's become an official war contractor and production switched from suits to uniforms, clothing nearly 25 per cent of the armed forces. Retail sales grew from £52,000 in 1915 to £150,000 in 1917, with a further £60,000 outstanding. In 1918 demob suits and bespoke suits were very much in demand.

What was to become a Burton's was opened on 17 September 1932, as a Lewis's department store – a store with a greater variety of goods then than any other in Leeds. Footfall on that opening day was over 100,000 people. 'Ask Me' girls were busy helping people navigate the 157 different departments, which sold everything from furniture to food. New features included escalators – the first to be installed in Leeds. The only item to run out that day were lobsters at 9*d* each.

Busy Burton's staff at the factory in Hudson Road, Harehills.

C

Chartists

Leeds was at the centre of the Chartist movement – the demand for the franchise to be extended to working-class men after the 1832 Reform Act. Feargus O'Connor, one of the leading Chartists, published *The Northern Star*, a Chartist propaganda sheet, in Leeds.

During the General Strike of 1842, Leeds's activism manifested itself in the Plug Riots when crowds of workers went from factory to factory pushing in the boiler plugs to wreck the boilers and bring production to a halt. Leeds Council was desperate, writing to the government in London that never before had Leeds experienced 'distress so universal, so prolonged, so exhaustive and so ruinous'. The local special constables were equipped with specially made 30,000 staves, curfews were imposed and pubs closed early. Hunslet, Holbeck and the west of the town saw rioting on 17 August, and an extra 1,600 special constables were sworn in and deployed to help the regulars. The 17th Lancers under Prince George of Cambridge and the Yorkshire Regiment under Lieutenant-Colonel William Beckett were mobilised in the town.

Mills at Farnley, Wortley and Pudsey had been 'plugged' and Armley was next. To meet the threat a huge force of police and military was deployed. First were the regular police

A Chartist riot. (Engraving from *True Stories of the Reign of Queen Victoria* by Cornelius Brown, 1886)

with cutlasses and heavy batons, followed by 1,200 special constables, three or four abreast with their staves. The army units brought up the rear: a troop of the 17th Lancers, eighteen men of the 187th Infantry (Yorkshire Regiment) bayonets fixed, a battery from the Royal Horse Artillery with gun and the Ripon Troop of Yeomanry. Meanwhile the mob had decommissioned Temple Mill in Holbeck. They were met by the Lancers and their weaponry. The Riot Act was read and the mob dispersed, only to reform at the Maclea and Marsh Mill in Dewsbury Road. Backup from the military was requested, but the specials made thirty-eight arrests before the army arrived. The police read the Riot Act again and the mob finally dispersed. Sentences included ten years' transportation.

City Varieties Music Hall

City Varieties began life in 1760 when the White Swan Coaching Inn was built in a yard off Briggate, appropriately known as the White Swan Yard. The White Swan featured a singing room upstairs, where various acts, though not drama, were staged. Charles Thornton became the licensee of the White Swan in 1857 and, after

City Palace of Varieties.

refurbishment, reopened in 1865 in the 2,000 seater as 'Thornton's New Music Hall and Fashionable Lounge'. It remains a rare surviving example of Victorian-era music halls of the 1850s and 1860s. Up against competition from the new Empire Theatre in Briggate in 1898, the theatre was sold to Fred Wood, who booked acts such as Charlie Chaplin, Lily Langtry and Laurel and Hardy. When Lily Langtry performed there, Edward VII would surreptitiously call on her. In gratitude for the theatre's discretion, he donated the crest that is now displayed above the auditorium.

Between 1913 and 1915 the theatre offered a challenge to local men to compete in wrestling matches. The Christmas pantomime of 1941, aptly *Babes in the Wood*, featured some unique audience participation when a woman in the audience (unexpectedly) gave birth to a 'healthy ginger-haired boy'. Harry Joseph, the owner, gave the baby boy free admission to the Varieties for life. Even less-conventional performances included the lady who hypnotised an alligator to music. In the 1950s striptease shows were put on, in which the girls were allowed to pose but not move. The year 1953 saw the start of the BBC's *The Good Old Days*, which ran for thirty years.

Leonora Cohen OBE

One of Leeds's most active women's champions was Leonora Cohen. Cohen (1873–1978) was a trade unionist, housewife and suffragette. She gained fame in 1913 when she tried to smash the glass showcase in the Tower of London Jewel House, which contained the insignia of the Order of Merit. A note wrapped around the iron bar she used read: 'This is my protest against the Governments treachery to the working

Leonora Cohen.

women of Great Britain.' After this she became known as the 'Tower Suffragette'. She was a bodyguard for Emmeline Pankhurst.

On this occasion she was wrestled to the ground by beefeaters. She was arrested on several more occasions and once went on a hunger and then a thirst strike while in custody in Armley Gaol. She was an active militant, organising protest marches on Woodhouse and Hunslet Moors. A photograph now in the Leeds City Archive was among her papers and bears the annotation in her handwriting: 'I, Leonora Cohen was arrested and charged with inciting the public to militancy under Edward 3rds act ("a trumped-up false charge") at the same period as George Lansbury and John Scurr. A protest meeting was held in Trafalgar Square, London for the release of the three charged, under the old Antediluvian Act.'

Leonora was born in 1873 in Hunslet. At fourteen, she was apprenticed to a city centre milliner working, as women were required to do, long hours without pay until she was upgraded to a probationer and paid 2*s* 6*d* a week. By sixteen she was promoted to head milliner and in her mid-twenties she had graduated to becoming a millinery buyer in Bridlington, where in 1900 she married jeweller Henry Cohen, much to the dismay of both families.

In 1911 Leonora was secretary of the Leeds branch of the militant Women's Social and Political Union. A demonstration in London, which ended in window-smashing and stone-throwing, saw Leonora incarcerated in Holloway for seven days. The Tower of London incident followed: she was so nervous before the attack that she went round twice on the Circle Line before entering the Tower. Afterwards, Leonora was put on trial, but acquitted on a technicality. Back in Leeds, Asquith's visit in November 1913 was incendiary: two suffragettes tried to set fire to the Headingly football stand, and violent demonstrations simmered around the Hippodrome where Asquith was to speak. Leonora was arrested for smashing windows and was sent to Armley Gaol.

Hostilities were put on hold for the duration of the war, and in February 1918 women over thirty were finally given the vote – better than nothing for the sterling support the women of Britain gave the country in its years of need. Women, however, had to wait another ten years before they finally gained full voting equality with men. By 1923, Cohen had become the first woman president of the Yorkshire Federation of Trades Councils that she served for twenty-five years. Her former house in Clarendon Road is marked by a blue plaque, and in 1928 she was awarded an OBE. She served as a Leeds magistrate for over thirty years. Leonora Cohen died at the age of 105.

The Corn Exchange

Corn has been formally traded in Leeds since the seventeenth century when the corn market was at the top of Briggate, between the Market Cross and New Street (now New Briggate). Growing trade led, in 1827, to the building of a corn exchange at the top of Briggate, but by the mid-nineteenth century this too proved too small.

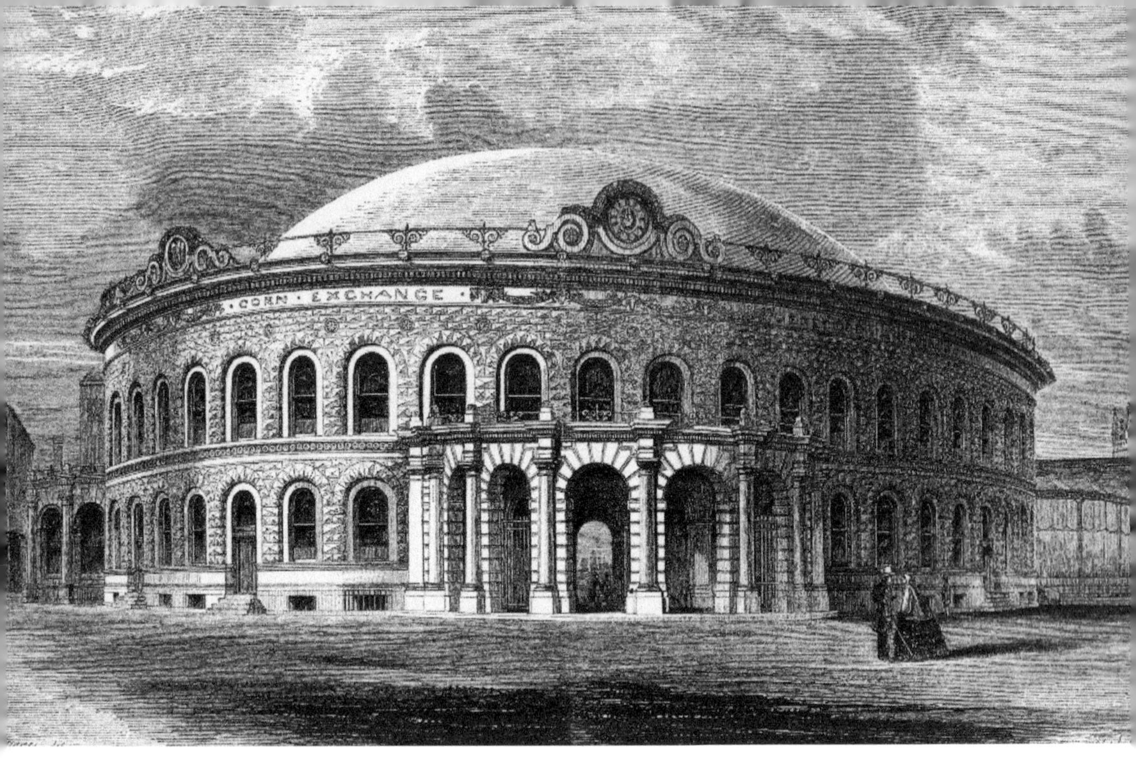

The 1860 Corn Exchange.

So, in 1860, a new corn exchange was proposed, to be designed and built along the lines of the state-of-the-art Edinburgh Corn Exchange. The Edinburgh exchange featured a large central space, in effect a trading floor, where farmers and corn factors transacted their business. The version at Leeds featured a large central space surrounded by fifty-six offices, accessed by arched doorways (some of them opened onto the street), while others opened into the interior of the building. Corn was stored in the huge basement area. It was also used as the headquarters of the fire brigade for a while. The building was a centre for the sale of corn wheat, barley, hops, peas, beans, seeds, oil cake and flour and hosted a farmers market and a regular leather fair.

Leeds Corn Exchange is one of just three corn exchanges in the country which still retain their original function as marketplaces, although not in the buying and selling of corn anymore.

An early image of the Corn Exchange.

Above, below and overleaf: Leeds Corn Exchange in 2015 and around 1920. (Courtesy of Civic Trust and Anita Morris Associates)

Corn was stored in the huge basement area. When it closed there were proposals to turn into a northern Albert Hall, but it was converted into a retail centre of some considerable splendour and reopened in 1990. The sympathetic renovation retained most of the original furnishings: merchants' desks, sample trays and name boards.

County Arcade (1907)

At the western end of County Arcade was The Bazaar, a two-storey emporium – the lower level selling meat and the upper level selling fancy goods and haberdashery. Men and women were segregated, with men downstairs and women upstairs – there was no chatting, no drinking or eating behind the counters and none of that

The magnificent County Arcade.

faddy wearing of bonnets by the women. County Arcade and Cross Arcade were built between 1898 and 1903 on the site of the White Horse Yard, creating a new street on each side of the arcade. Wood Street became Queen Victoria Street, and Cheapside became King Edward Street on the site of the New Shambles and the Fish Market. The vaulted ceiling is glass with three domes, displaying mosaic figures representing Liberty, Commerce, Labour and Art. Lyons Café, at the end, was previously known as the Carlton Café and the Ceylon Café.

Above left and right, below left and right: Four more views of the County Arcade.

Daniel Defoe

Daniel Defoe, in his *A Tour Through the Whole Island of Great Britain*, provides a meticulously detailed description of the Leeds wool trade, abbreviated here:

> The encrease of the manufacturers and of the trade, soon made the market too great to be confined to the brigg or bridge, and it is now kept in the High-street, beginning from the bridge, and running up north almost to the market-house, where the ordinary market for provisions begins, which also is the greatest of its kind in all the north of England, except Hallifax ... There are for this purpose a set of travelling merchants in Leeds, who go all over England with droves of pack horses, and to all the fairs and market towns over the whole island ... they supply the shops by wholesale or whole pieces; and not only so, but give large credit too ...; 'tis ordinary for one of these men to carry a thousand pounds value of cloth with them at a time ... warehouse-keepers not only supply all the shop-keepers and wholesale men in London, but sell also very great quantities to the merchants, as well for exportation to the English colonies ... especially New England, New York, Virginia, &. as also to the Russiamerchants, who send an exceeding quantity to Petersburgh, Riga, Dantzic, Narva, and to Sweden and Pomerania.

The Dark Arches (1846), Granary Wharf

One of the most significant changes in Leeds in the latter half of the nineteenth century was caused by the coming of the railway and the construction of Wellington station and New station over the river, and the northern part of the canal basin. Wellington station dates from 1846. Between 1866 and 1869 the North Eastern Railway constructed New station to connect lines from Bradford and the west and lines to York, Selby and the north-east.

The station was, amazingly, built over a series of arches spanning the Aire, Neville Street and Swinegate. This magnificent edifice – the Dark Arches – can

The River Aire looking towards the Dark Arches.

still be seen and enjoyed today. More than 18 million bricks were used in their construction, a record at the time, in what was a series of independent viaducts two or four tracks wide. The station is at the terminus of the Leeds & Liverpool Canal, but as it is raised high above ground level you can access to the Dark Arches from the towpath.

At first the arches were used for storage, some of them by soap manufacturers Joseph Watson & Sons, to store resin, oil and tallow. Unfortunately, in 1892 these inventories, the bridge and railway line over the canal basin were destroyed in a fire. The bridge was rebuilt, and the line restored in just five and a half days.

Joseph Watson & Sons and their Whitehall Soap Works was one of the largest soap works in England, employing around 750 people and manufacturing 600 tons of soap a week in 1893. Famous brands included Watson's Matchless Cleanser and Venus Soap. The firm was known as 'Soapy Joe's'. They also made glycerine for dynamite production and traded in hides and skins. Watson's was sold to Lever's in 1917, and became Elida Gibbs in 1971, closing in 1987 when the company moved to Seacroft.

The East Leeds Military Hospital, Beckett Street

The date of 17 September 1914 was a pivotal one for Leeds. That was the day on which the first convoy of eighty wounded soldiers arrived back in their home city at the old Midland station. They were casualties from the Battle of the Marne; few of them were able to walk and many sported injuries too terrible to describe. A sombre crowd of 6,000 or so Leeds people looked on as the soldiers were taken from the City Square to Beckett's Park. They showered the troops with cigarettes and tobacco.

The old Leeds Union Workhouse in Beckett Street (St James's Hospital in 1925) had been converted in 1915 into a 500-bed hospital for just that 17 September eventuality and rebadged the East Leeds War Hospital. There was a branch hospital at Killingbeck and medical facilities at Gledhow Hall and Harehills Council School.

With No. 2 Northern General, it treated over 57,000 patients throughout the war. After 1917, East Leeds took on the administrative role originally based at Beckett's Park; it was also the first specialist dental unit in the country. Dentures for the entire Northern Command were fitted here and new methods in oral surgery and jaw reconstruction were developed.

Ambulances at the ready in 1917. (From the George Sprittles's scrapbook, courtesy of and © Leeds Beckett University)

Above left: The Cheerio Boys providing entertainment in 1918. (From the George Sprittles's scrapbook. Courtesy of and © Leeds Beckett University)

Above right: Maxillofacial workshop at the hospital, 1916. (From the George Sprittles's scrapbook. Courtesy of and © Leeds Beckett University)

Below: Flat-roof ward, 1917. (From the George Sprittles's scrapbook. Courtesy of and © Leeds Beckett University)

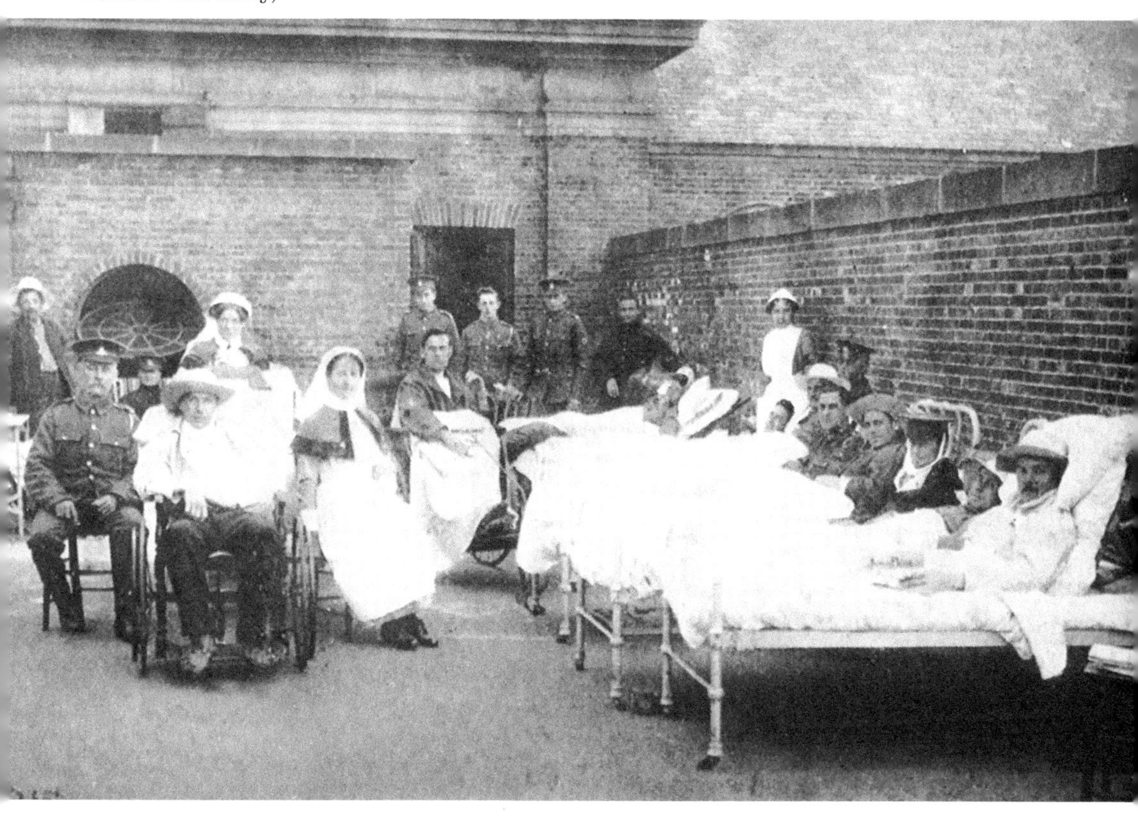

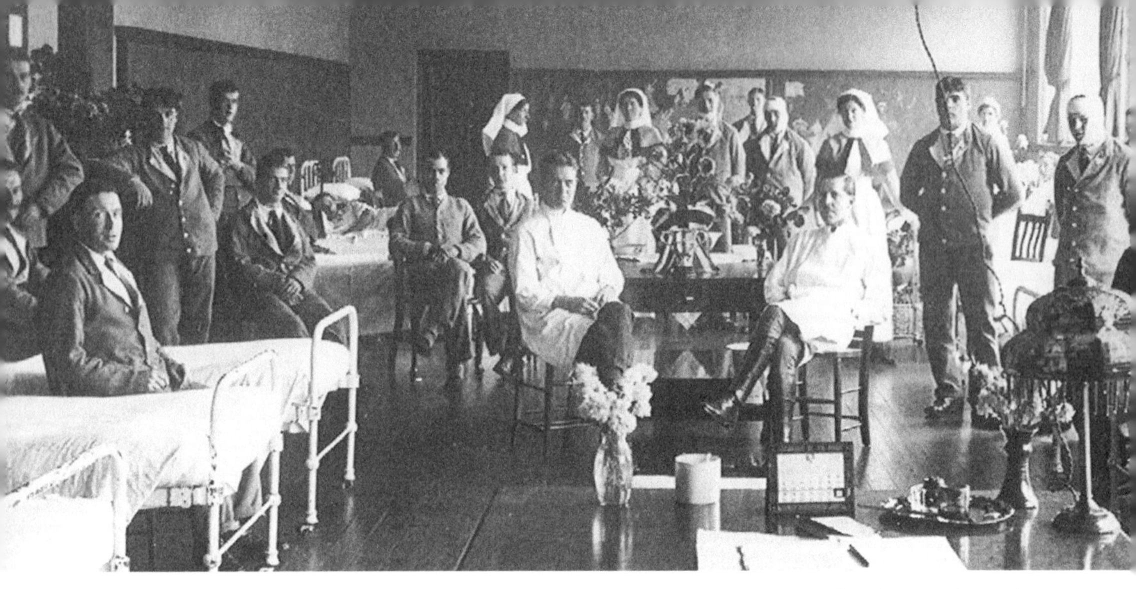

The Jaw Ward in 1916. (From the George Sprittles's scrapbook. Courtesy of and © Leeds Beckett University)

Private George Edward Ellison

Private George Edward Ellison (1878 to 11 November 1918) has the unfortunate honour of being the last British soldier to be killed in action in the First World War. He died at 9.30 a.m., a mere ninety minutes before the Armistice was signed, while on a patrol outside Mons, Belgium. He was born and lived in Leeds, joining the army as a regular soldier only to leave in 1912 when he married Hannah Maria Burgan and became a coal miner. Just before the outbreak of war he was recalled to the army, joining the 5th Royal Irish Lancers. He fought at the Battle of Mons in 1914, the first Ypres, Lens, Loos and Cambrai, among others. He is buried in the St Symphorien Military Cemetery, south-east of Mons.

Tragically, the Allies and Germany had signed the Armistice, ending the war, six hours earlier, but delayed its coming into effect until 11 a.m. so that the message could be conveyed to troops at the front. This delay cost Ellison his life. He was one of 11,000 casualties, dead and wounded, on that last morning. By bizarre coincidence – because Mons was lost to the British at the very beginning of the war and regained at the very end – his grave faces that of John Parr, the first British soldier to be killed during the First World War.

International Military Cemetery (English and German) and British memorial of Saint-Symphorien (Mons). (Photographer: Jean-Pol Grandmont)

F

Mr and Mrs Horace Fawcett

Mr and Mrs Horace Fawcett relax in their 'air-raid shelter' in October 1940 in Cardigan Avenue, Burley, which was actually a very comfortable reinforced coal cellar. The Leodis website tells that 'the Fawcetts were held up as a shining example of resourcefulness and ingenuity. When members of the ARP came to inspect this shelter, they found the walls neatly papered, electric lighting and a heater installed, chairs and a table, and pictures on the wall, with a cot for the baby in the corner. "It is a grand piece of work" was the comment of Cllr. HW Sellars, ARP chairman'. Many others just moaned about their shelters.

How very British ... 'a shining example of resourcefulness and ingenuity'. (Courtesy of Leodis. © Leeds Library & Information Services)

This waymarker is carved with Fiennes's image. It is in No Man's Heath, near where she was almost mugged – the only time in around thirty years of travel that this happened. Riding to Whitchurch in Cheshire, she records that she was harassed by two 'fellows' who she thought had pistols. Fortunatly for Fiennes, it was market day in Whitchurch and, as she approached the town, the crowds scared off the highwaymen.

Celia Fiennes

The fearless Celia Fiennes called in at Leeds on her trip around Britain and, although she seems more preoccupied with the price and strength of beer and whether her cheese sandwich should be on the house or not, she does give us an intriguing contemporary picture of the town in her 1698 *Through England On a Side Saddle in the Time of William and Mary*:

> Leeds is a Large town, severall Large streetes, Cleane and well pitch'd and good houses all built of stone. Some have good Gardens and Steps up to their houses and walls before them. This is Esteemed the Wealthyest town of its bigness in the Country its manufacture is ye woollen Cloth-the Yorkshire Cloth in wch they are all Employ'd and are Esteemed very Rich and very proud ... here if one Calls for a tankard of Ale wch is allwayes a groate its the only dear thing all over Yorkshire, their ale is very strong ... but for paying this Groat for your ale you may have a slice of meate Either hott or Cold according to the tyme of day you Call, or Else butter and Cheese Gratis into the bargaine ...

Isabella Ford

Isabella Ormston Ford (1855–1924) was a social reformer, suffragist and writer on socialism, feminism and workers' rights. She was born in Adel Grange in Adel, the youngest of eight children in a pacifist Quaker family. Ford felt compelled to resign from the National Union of Women's Suffrage Societies over the vexed issue of their support for the war. She then concentrated on working toward peace and founded the Leeds branch of the Women's Peace Crusade.

G

Richard Gaukroger

Richard Gaukroger, thirty-one, lived with his wife, Harriet, on the York Road in east Leeds. Richard spent much of his time in the pub, a pursuit for which he was constantly harangued by Harriet. In time he grew tired of this and decided he wanted to spend the rest of his life with another woman; she was called Poll. He raised this with Harriet, who responded by raising the poker to him and threatening him with it. Richard was smoking a pipe at the time and snapped, dashing across the room and ramming the pipe stem up into her nose. Harriet gingerly withdrew the pipe, which resulted in extreme pain and profuse bleeding. For his part, Richard reclaimed the pipe and resumed smoking it. Unfortunately, over the next few days, Harriet deteriorated and then died. The post-mortem showed a fragment of the pipe lodged in her skull; her cause of death was inflammation of the brain. Richard Gaukroger was convicted of manslaughter and received twenty-one months in jail.

Greenwood & Batley

During the Crimean War (1853–56) the engineering firm of Greenwood & Batley won the contract to make machines for weapon manufacture for the arsenals at Woolwich and the Royal Small Arms Factory, Enfield. At the end of the war the company also participated, fittingly enough, in staging the illuminations in Leeds to celebrate the victory. Fairburn Greenwood & Batley provided 'a brilliant device in gas consisting of lines of gas along the architecture of the Grecian façade and enclosing two large stars and, V and N in large Roman capitals'.

In August 1856 the great and the good of Leeds entertained Lord Cardigan, leader of the Charge of the Light Brigade in the Crimean War, in the banqueting hall of the Stock Exchange in Leeds. The 'People of Yorkshire' presented him with a sword that cost £250. Nineteenth-century foreign politics and diplomacy were never strong points at Greenwood & Batley. 'Arms and the (wrong) man' might have been an appropriate company motto.

During the American Civil War (1861–65) Greenwood & Batley were happily supplying arms to the Confederates: 'It appears that in this case certain goods were manufactured by the plaintiffs, Thos. Greenwood and John Batley, carrying on business under the name or style of Greenwood and Batley, of Leeds for the Confederate States of America, at a time when they were recognized by this country as belligerents.'

In February 1878 they faced 'an action brought by General Berdan of the United States, America, to recover from the defendants, who are engineers and machinists, carrying on business and having manufactories at Leeds, a sum of £5,500 odd, by way of commission on orders relating to the manufacture of guns for the Russian Government'. Russia and the USA were not at war at the time; however, Hiram Berdan claimed that Greenwood & Batley had supplied machines to produce his 'Berdan Rifle' in the Russian Tula factory and that he was therefore owed commission. The Berdan Rifle became standard issue to the Russian army from 1869 to 1891.

The Griffin (1872), Boar Lane

The pub is on the site of the earlier Griffin Hotel, a coaching inn from at least the seventeenth century. It was rebuilt as a railway hotel for the Leeds New station, which opened in 1869 and was owned by the joint London & North West and North East railways. The Gothic Revival building boasted a unique Potts clock at the corner of the building with the hours ingeniously replaced by the words 'Griffin Hotel'. For many, though, the Griffin will be cherished as the place where Leeds United was born.

Underneath the arches in the Griffin today.

H

Tony Harrison (b. 1937)

Poet, translator and playwright Tony Harrison was born on Tempest Road, south Leeds, and started his education at Cross Flatts county primary school, Beeston. He later won a scholarship to Leeds Grammar School, where he found the tension between his working-class background and the grammar school environment hard to come to terms with. He alludes to this in his poetry, not least in his most anthologised poem 'Them & [uz]', which recalls the occasion at Leeds Grammar when he was forbidden to recite Keats because of his accent. 'Them & [uz]' asserts 'We'll occupy/ your lousy leasehold Poetry', and reveals that in Wordsworth 'matter/water are full rhymes' – thus laying the groundwork for his ongoing attack on the cultural barriers that divide the classes.

Street cricket, Victoria Place, Little London, Leeds, 1954. (© Marc Riboud)

Harrison went on to Leeds University where he studied Classics. His work includes the controversial, but critically, acclaimed poem 'V' (set at his parents' grave in a Leeds cemetery 'now littered with beer cans and vandalised by obscene graffiti') and 'The Trackers of Oxyrhynchus' (1990). There is also fine translations of Aeschylus' *Oresteia'* and Aristophanes' *Lysistrata*, Molière's *The Misanthrope*, and *The Mysteries* (1985), an adaptation of the English medieval mystery plays based on the York and Wakefield Cycles. He told Melvyn Bragg in 2012 that 'it was only when I did the Mystery Plays and got Northern actors doing verse, that I felt that I was reclaiming the energy of classical verse in the voices that it was created for'.

Harrison's upbringing in working-class Leeds, with its urban, industrial landscape, had a clear influence on his work. In the poem 'Shrapnel' he links the blitz of his boyhood to the London bombers of 7 July 2005, who came from the same part of Beeston where he grew up.

Simon Armitage has written in the *New Statesman* how he was 'impressed with the way [Harrison] deals with his upbringing and background in his poems, and more specifically, his accent'. 'Who'd have thought,' says Armitage, 'that some of t'most moving poems in t'language would have been composed in a form of English normally reserved for sheep-sha**ers and colliers?' To Mary Kaiser in *World Literature Today* Harrison's 'central poetic concern is with a distinctly British problem'. Harrison has a 'predominant fascination with social and class conflict', stated Kaiser, who noted that 'throughout his work the dynamic of an overlooked minority resisting an elite and powerful majority plays itself out, whether the context is ancient Greece or Rome, the postwar Leeds of his childhood, or contemporary London'. In Harrison's first major anthology of poetry, *The Loiners* (1970), the author 'explored his relationship with the eponymous citizens of the working-class community of Leeds ... from childhood encounters with sex in Leeds ...'

Richard Hoggart (1918–2014)

The impoverished Potternewton area of Leeds is where Richard Hoggart grew up – one of three children in a very poor family. His soldier father was a housepainter and veteran of both the Boer War and the First World War. He died of brucellosis when Hoggart was one year old. His mother died when he was eight. He later spoke movingly and poignantly about his family's abject poverty: 'When I see – or see film of – a driven bird flying to its nest and anxiously, earnestly feeding the open mouths, the image of our mother comes to mind ... When you have seen a woman standing frozen, while tears start slowly down her cheeks because a sixpence has been lost ... you do not easily forget.'

Such experience was to inform Hoggart's work. The eight year old was then raised by a loving, widowed grandmother in Hunslet, in a typically overcrowded cottage – its one claim to fame being that it was the only mains-connected cottage in the street.

Central Leeds slums.

Working-class Leeds, May 1954.

Betting shop in the Turk's Head Yard, off Briggate, 1954. (© Marc Riboud)

The perceptive and indomitable aunt Ethel, a tailor, lived there too. She focussed on young Richard when a head teacher picked him out as a pupil with promise. Ethel quickly realised that this might be Richard's chance to escape the shackles restricting him to his class. She urged him to concentrate on his education, the result of which saw him follow big brother Tom to Cockburn High School, a grammar school, assisted by hardship grants from the Board of Guardians and the Royal British Legion. He failed the eleven-plus maths paper, but won a scholarship thanks to his English essay, supported by a plea from his junior school head teacher to remark his paper. Hoggart later discovered that his coveted scholarship was one of only thirty available at the time for a catchment of 65,000 children of his age. This 'close-thing' experience inculcated a lifelong support for comprehensive education.

Hoggart also never forgot the gratitude he owed to his extended family for inspiring him; he never forgot how fortunate he was to win that rare scholarship. Putting his earlier maths failure behind him, he gained the equivalent of a distinction in O-level maths. He then won a scholarship to study English at the University of Leeds in 1936, from which he graduated with a first. Again, sheer hard work was the key to his success. In his obituary of Hoggart (in *The Guardian*, Thursday 10 April 2014) John Ezard wrote: 'While Cockburn grammar school eventually took the boy out of Hunslet, he never let it take Hunslet out of the boy.'

The book for which Hoggart is most famous, the classic *The Uses of Literacy: Aspects of Working Class Life*, was published in 1957. It is partly autobiographical, drawing on his youthful experience of working-class life and has been seen as a detailed first-hand account of the loss of Britain's authentic working-class popular culture, deploring the tidal wave of a mass culture through post-war advertising, the influences of mass-media and Americanisation that had arrived in the mid- to late 1940s. These modish concepts, Hoggart observed, were to change British urban working-class people forever – their lives, their urban landscape, values and culture.

Of course, *The Uses of Literacy* was just one of many works produced by Richard Hoggart. It is probably safe to assume that most if not all were influenced by the urban landscape and its people, which Hoggart met every day in Potternewton and Hunslet.

Hyde Park Picture House

The 1914 opening was promoted by an advertisement in the *Yorkshire Evening Post*, which, amid all the war news, heralded the new picture house as 'The Cosiest in Leeds'. Apart from patriotic films, the picture house also showed newsreels of the war to the people of Leeds, anxious to learn about the 6,000 men from Leeds who had enlisted. They were reliant on the picture house news because many of them could not read the newspapers or afford a wireless. The Empire and Hippodrome also showed war news and at the Empire the audiences stood up at the end to the French and Russian national anthems, in addition to usual 'God Save the King' and 'Rule Britannia'.

Hyde Park Picture House and ornate lamp standard.

Above: Interior. (© Ollie Jenkins)

Right: Exterior. (© Ollie Jenkins)

I

The Infirmary at Leeds

The General Infirmary at Leeds (its old official name) goes back to June 1767 when an Infirmary 'for the relief of the sick and hurt poor within this parish' was set up in a private house in Kirkgate. Four years later the General Infirmary's first purpose-built building opened near City Square in Infirmary Street, on the site of the former Yorkshire Bank – the five founding physicians were all graduates of the University of Edinburgh Medical School. LGI has continued to expand ever since, resulting initially in the move to an impressive new site on Great George Street in 1869. The magnificent infirmary buildings here were designed by Sir George Gilbert Scott.

Finsen Light Room.

The LGI in Great George Street.

I

The Finsen Light Room at Leeds General Infirmary was established in 1901 when a dermatology department was established at the hospital. The Finsen lamp was developed by Danish physician Niels Ryberg Finsen who discovered the therapeutic effects of ultraviolet rays for certain conditions of the skin – in particular lupus vulgaris, a tuberculous skin disease. The treatment was successful and by 1903 three lamps were in use with sixty patients a day being treated.

A ward in the LGI.

Al fresco paediatrics at the LGI.

Operating theatre at the LGI in the 1950s.

Jewish Persecution in Leeds – Leeds's own Kristallnacht

The night of 3–4 June 1917 saw the outbreak of ugly scenes of anti-Jewish violence in the Jewish quarter of Leeds: Bridge Street, North Street and Regent Street. Street fighting led to the vandalism and looting of Jewish premises and businesses, and Jewish soldiers were attacked. The police were accused of complacency. It had obviously escaped the notice of the perpetrators that of the 25,000 or so Jews in Leeds at the time, 2,500 had enlisted for military service, and that is despite the exemptions for those engaged in war work such as tailoring. There were Oswald Mosely rallies in Leeds in 1936.

Kirkstall Brewery (1833), Broad Lane, Kirkstall

Kirkstall Brewery is synonymous in some ways with twelfth-century Cistercian Kirkstall Abbey. Indeed, Yorkshire's first pub was the alehouse in which Samuel Ellis started brewing in AD 953 at Bardsey to the north of Leeds. It is still there under the guise of the Priest's Inn and then of the Bingley Arms, but it is significant to us because of the Kirkstall Abbey monks who drank there on the way to St Mary's Abbey in York. Not only did they refresh themselves on their journeys, but they brewed ale at the abbey itself – you might call this the first Kirkstall Brewery.

Kirkstall Brewery.

Our Kirkstall Brewery operated between 1833 and 1983 when it was closed by Whitbread. The brewery buildings have been well preserved and now provide accommodation for 1,000 or so Leeds Beckett University students at what is now Kirkstall Brewery Student Village. This project was undertaken by the then Leeds Metropolitan (now Beckett) University. A new Kirkstall Brewery has been established nearby with many echoes of the original: the old brewery crest, product names and even their flagship 6 per cent beer, Dissolution Extra IPA, brewed from an original export beer from the 1860s.

The original buildings are Grade II listed, built on either side of the Leeds & Liverpool Canal. You can still see on one of the buildings on the west side of the canal, The Warehouse, the doors just above the water level that were used to load beer barrels onto barges. By 1898 the brewery was producing around 72,000 barrels of beer a year, sold locally and as far away as Australia and New Zealand. Dutton's Blackburn Brewery Ltd purchased Kirkstall Brewery Co. Ltd and its subsidiaries, Albion Brewery (Leeds) Ltd and Willow Brewery Co. Ltd in 1936 and later renamed it as Dutton's Lancashire & Yorkshire Brewery Corporation Ltd. Dutton's was bought by Whitbread in 1957. Kirkstall Brewery was refurbished while the production of bitter and mild went up to quarter of a million barrels a year.

A fascinating revelation was made during renovation of the buildings when it was discovered that a Second World War submarine engine was installed at the brewery as power backup. This engine was one of a pair built in 1943, but was never actually installed in a submarine. The size of a Ford Transit van, it was sold in 1948 to the brewery and now resides at the Anson Engine Museum in Poynton, Cheshire, being restored.

L

Leeds City Museum (1819), Park Row

The museum began life in 1819, established on Park Row by the Leeds Philosophical and Literary Society and opened to the public in 1821. In 1941, the museum building and many displays and artefacts were badly damaged by bombing. The museum closed in 1965 but reopened in 2008 in the refurbished Mechanics' Institute Building. One of the most popular exhibits is the infamous 'Leeds Tiger'. It was saved from the curators' skip by the *Yorkshire Post* when it mounted a successful campaign to retain it as a popular centrepiece of the museum's collection.

The Leeds Tiger was originally a tiger-skin rug when presented to the museum in the nineteenth century; the tiger had been shot for taking an unhealthy interest in the occupants of a village in India. The pelt was then sewn with other tiger skins and, instead of being mounted properly, it was stuffed rather amateurishly with straw. The reputation of and affection for the tiger, meanwhile, escalated. From being just a curious observer of Indian village life it was lionised and elevated to the legendary status of a serial killer of forty villagers.

'Roarrrr!'

The Leeds 'Wizard'

William Dove, a young tenant farmer and a Methodist from Newby Wiske, just north of Thirsk, was tried and executed in 1856 for poisoning his wife Harriet. The trial was complicated by the fact that Dove had been involved with Henry Harrison, a Leeds 'wizard'. Harrison exhibited through words and actions a strong affinity for magic and satanic powers, all of which was used in an attempt to prove Dove's insanity. Dove, it seems, murdered his wife to realise a tempting prediction made by Harrison that he would remarry a better-looking and wealthy woman. Dove engaged Harrison to perform various acts of magic and made a written pact with the Devil.

The Dove-Harrison relationship started soon after Dove moved to industrial, cholera-ridden Leeds with his new wife after failing as a farmer. The marriage was hardly stable and Harrison identified the couple as vulnerable sorts he could exploit. Pseudo-medicine and poisons were the stock-in trade of such charlatans as Harrison, along with a considerable spoonful of duplicity and lies. He 'prescribed' strychnine to see off Harriet Dove. Her husband was tried at the summer assizes in York and hanged on St George's Field, opposite the castle.

The Leopard, Briggate

A popular haunt of clothiers from Farsely. Defoe describes the importance of pubs to the clothing industry in Leeds. He informs us that the cloth market was a swift

The Leopard Hotel.

early morning affair, starting at 7 a.m., and was all over by 9 a.m. when it was time for a good breakfast, which was taken at public houses near the bridge. These meals were called Brig-End-Shots, which, according to Ralph Thoresby, 'The clothier may, together with his Pot of Ale, have a Noggin o' Pottage, and a Trencher of either Boil'd or Roast Beef for two Pence.'

The Leeds Blitz

Throughout the Second World War seventy-seven Leeds people were killed and 197 buildings were destroyed with 7,623 damaged, and subsequently repaired, in nine raids and eighty-seven air-raid alerts. There were twenty-four major fires. Leeds firefighters were comparatively underworked and sent crews to deal with fires in London, Liverpool, York, Coventry, Sheffield, Birmingham and Hull where the bombing was, York apart, much heavier.

On 1–2 September 1940, between 3,000 and 4,000 incendiaries and fourteen high-explosive bombs were dropped on the city. The night of 14–15 March 1941 saw Leeds's most devastating raid, the so-called 'Quarter Blitz' after the tonnage of bombs dropped. In Morley there was damage to property in Spenslea Grove, Homefield Avenue and Model Road. Casualties included one fatal, and four injured. In the city centre incendiaries fell on Aire Street; the Town Hall and City Museum were badly damaged, partially destroying the Law Library in the Town Hall and some of the Egyptology collection in the museum. Kirkstall power station was a target.

Below left: How the Luftwaffe neatly converted this semi-detached house into a detached one on 22 September 1941 in a cul-de-sac off Cliff Road. (Courtesy of Leodis. © Leeds Library & Information Services)

Below right: Washing day in East Grove Street, Burmantofts – probably a Monday. (Courtesy of Leodis. © Marc Riboud 1954 and Leeds Library & Information Services)

The Hepworth Arcade and the streets around Water Lane were alight. By midnight Mill Hill Chapel, the Royal Exchange Building, Denby & Spink's furniture store and the *Yorkshire Post* building had been hit. These were followed by bombs at Gipton, Headingley, Woodhouse and Roundhay roads. There was further damage at Fairbairn

Left: A bomb-damaged Marsh Lane station on 1 September 1940.

Below: Some serious bomb damage in Easterly Road on 2 September 1940.

Right: Hitler coming down Briggate, but not how he would have chosen to.

Below: A mobile First Aid post.

Lawson's, Greenwood & Batleys, Wellington Street, Wellington Road goods yard and Central and City stations. The infirmary, Town Hall, City Museum, Kirkgate Market, St Peter's School, Park Square, Hotel Metropole and Quarry Hill flats were also hit.

A total of 25 tons of bombs fell on Leeds during the raid – a quarter of the 100 tons used as the threshold to qualify as a 'major raid'. This was bad enough, but to put it into perspective by comparison that same night in Glasgow 203 aircraft dropped 231 tons of high explosives and 1,650 incendiaries, while in Sheffield 117 aircraft dropped 83 tons of high explosives and 328 incendiaries. The bombers over Leeds were probably Junkers Ju-88s and Dornier Do-17s if those shot down in other parts of Yorkshire that night are anything to go by.

The Leeds International Piano Competition

The prestigious Leeds International Piano Competition, also known as The Leeds and formerly the Leeds International Pianoforte Competition, happens every three years in the Great Hall of the University of Leeds and in Leeds Town Hall. It was founded in 1961 by Marion, Countess of Harewood, Fanny Waterman, and Roslyn Lyons, with the first competition in 1963. Since 2003, the competitors have been accompanied by the Hallé Orchestra, under the leadership of Mark Elder.

Leeds Workhouse

In theory, the workhouse was intended to provide care and comfort to the most needy and shield them from the worst depredations of life. The reality was often very different.

The building now housing the Thackray Medical Museum opened in 1861 as the first purpose-built Leeds Union Workhouse to accommodate 784 paupers. Over time new buildings were added to the workhouse, including a separate infirmary. In 1848, the Leeds Guardians built the Moral and Industrial Training Schools on the north side of Beckett Street. During the First World War it was called the East Leeds War Hospital, caring for armed services personnel. In 1925 the Leeds Union Workhouse infirmary was repurposed and renamed St James's Hospital.

Leeds Union Workhouse from the cemetery – the last resting place of many paupers. (© St James's Hospital, Leeds)

M

Makkah Masjid (2003), Thornville Road

The stunning Leeds Makkah Masjid is one of the main masajid in Leeds, serving the Muslim communities of Headingley, Hyde Park, the universities and surrounding areas. The mosque suddenly appears out of the surrounding terraced streets. It arose from a dire need to accommodate the burgeoning Muslim community locally.

After much opposition from the council, planning permission was finally given to build a new mosque on the site of a dilapidated Christadelphian church that had been redundant for many years. This was a unique church constructed with wooden structure and was a registered listed building – hence the opposition.

Above and right: Two views of the stunning mosque.

Leeds Makkah Masjid was finally opened on 29 August 2003 at a cost of £1.8 million and after a truly magnificent response to an appeal for funds. The mosque reflects classical Arabic and Persian influences and is decorated on the outside with attractive blue, green and cream tiles. The magnificent dome inside features more calligraphy than any other mosque in the UK. It was produced by the famous Pakistani calligrapher Naveed Bhatti and comprises the ninety-nine names of Allah and Muhammad, the names of the famous companions, various verses from the holy Quran and a complete chapter (Chapter 55).

The building has three floors and can hold over 2,700 people. It has three minarets and the dome. There are two main halls for men and another for women. The mosque also has rooms for computers and a library.

Marks & Spencer

The business started out as a Penny Bazaar at Kirkgate Market in 1884. In March 2013, M&S opened a stall at Kirkgate Market in the same place that Michael Marks opened the first Penny Bazaar stall in 1884. The M&S heritage stall and coffee shop is beside the famous M&S clock in the 1904 Kirkgate Market building and marks the starting point of the M&S Heritage Trail. In 2012, the magnificent M&S Company Archive relocated to the Michael Marks Building, Western Campus, University of Leeds.

The birthplace of Marks & Spencer is commemorated in the new image.

The Mechanics' Institute

Leeds Mechanics' Institute (1824) was built by Cuthbert Broderick. The objective of the Mechanics' Institutes was to furnish a technical education for the working man and for professionals to 'address societal needs by incorporating fundamental scientific thinking and research into engineering solutions'. They effectively transformed science and technology education for the man in the street. A number of them have become cutting-edge universities. The world's first opened in Edinburgh in 1821 as the School of Arts of Edinburgh, later Heriot-Watt University. This was followed in 1823 by the institute in Glasgow, which was founded on the site of the institution set up in 1800 by George Birkbeck and the Andersonian University offering free lectures on arts, science and technical subjects. It moved to London in 1804, became the London Mechanics' Institute from 1823 and, later, Birkbeck College. Liverpool opened in July 1823 and Manchester (later to become UMIST) in 1824. By 1850, there were over 700 Mechanics' Institutes in the UK and abroad, many of which developed into libraries, colleges and universities. Mechanics' Institutes provided free lending libraries and also offered lectures, laboratories, and occasionally, as with Glasgow, a museum.

Leeds is a case in point. In 1846, the Leeds Mechanics' Institute was already offering drawing classes when it merged with the Literary Institute, creating Leeds School of Art. In 1868 Leeds Mechanics Institute becomes the Leeds Institute of Science, Art, and Literature. In 1903, it moved to the Vernon Street building, whose radical design reflected the Arts and Crafts movement. Henry Moore and Barbara Hepworth are among the alumni, enrolling in 1919 and 1920, respectively. By 1946, fifteen past students had subsequently been appointed as principals of schools of art. Over time, new design departments were established, including furniture, graphic design and

Leeds City Museum on opening day, 22 February 2009. (Courtesy of Andrew Roberts)

printmaking. A new pottery and workshops were built, and in 1959 a new library was opened. In the mid-1980s the Blenheim Walk building was built.

Today the Mechanics' Institute, as we have seen, hosts Leeds City Museum, resplendent with its marvellous interior – the circular central hall, originally a lecture room with balcony and Ionic columns, has its floor raised on cast-iron columns. This, 'the Albert Hall', was designed to accommodate up to 1,500 people and was lit by clerestory windows. Around the perimeter was a library, reading room, workshops and studios, classrooms (including one set aside for moral instruction) and dining rooms.

When the Mechanics' Institute stopped educating, it became a concert hall, known as the Civic Theatre, and later the City Museum.

Kathleen Mumford

A tragic mercy killing. The sad case of Derek Mumford, classified as a 'mental defective', is one of the earliest cases of euthanasia. He was completely disabled and was never be able to help himself in any way. Despite strenuous efforts to have her son properly treated, which included carrying him 5 miles twice a day for a number of weeks from their home in Middleton, south Leeds, Kathleen Mumford was sentenced to death for murder after she gassed Derek in the oven. The press headlined this as 'Murder of Imbecile Son'. She gave Derek sixteen Luminal tablets (the anti-epileptic drug phenobarbital), gassed him and carried him wrapped in a blanket to Leeds Town Hall. He died later in Leeds Infirmary where she tried to prevent attempts to resuscitate him.

Kathleen Mumford had been beside herself and, rightly, could see no dignified or worthwhile future for her son who suffered from Little's disease, a form of cerebral palsy. The best she could get from the authorities was that Derek should be admitted to a 'mental colony' for the rest of his life. Kathleen Mumford knew that this was not the answer and even asked her GP if she could 'do away with the boy'. She knew what she was talking about and wanted to spare him from the abuse and mistreatment she herself had suffered while being raised in a Victorian orphanage in Spennymoor.

Kathleen Mumford was duly convicted of murder. To the judge it was quite simple, murder was murder even though Mumford insisted that she had no regrets regarding her action because she knew that this was the humane thing to do: 'He would never be normal ... what was the child to live for? All the days of his life he would have been an imbecile. Was it right that a child should have to live like that? Therefore I ended his sufferings.'

The jury found her guilty of wilful murder, but with 'the very strongest recommendation to mercy'. After two years in Aylesbury Prison she was released on pardon and returned to her home town of Darlington. In 2015, a powerful short film based on these events was released: *An Unfortunate Woman*.

N

The Northern Area Army Clothing Depot

The Army Clothing Depot opened in Swinegate, Leeds, near to what was then the Midland Railway station in King's Mills, next to what was originally the Tramways Depot. The War Office requisitioned and adapted it for the 'handling of pieces of khaki cloth and uniforms'. By May 1915 more storage space was needed so the cattle market buildings in Gelderd Road were taken over to store cloth – up to 9 million yards of it. A total of 3 million uniforms were also stored in another depot, belonging to the Aire & Calder Navigation.

A British army infantryman of the First World War in the Royal Armouries Museum, Leeds.

A Park Row premises saw 80,000 shirts inspected every week. All told, the Northern Area produced 53 million shirts, 21 million pairs of army trousers, 8 million pairs of cavalry trousers, 10 million greatcoats, 24 million puttees, 89 million pairs of socks and 30 million pairs of boots. Apart from production and inspection, the depots also recycled uniforms and other clothing salvaged from battlefield casualties.

Before the Leeds depot opened the system for uniform manufacture and provision was cumbersome to say the least. Hitherto, cloth produced in northern mills was sent by rail to the Central Army Clothing Depot in Pimlico, London, where it was checked and tested, then sent back to Yorkshire for making up. The new Leeds depot, with its 150 staff, revolutionised the process and answered the endless need for more and more uniforms; it enabled cloth to be processed locally in a timely fashion. By the end of the war some 750,000 uniforms per week were passing through Leeds, some of which was produced by Edwin Woodhouse & Co. Ltd in Farsley.

No. 2 Northern General, Beckett's Park

The No. 2 Northern Hospital in Leeds had affiliated hospitals in Harrogate, Cookridge, Lotherton Hall, Armley, Stokesley, Northallerton and Thirsk. It was a Territorial Force hospital based in the converted teacher training college, City of Leeds Training College, at Beckett's Park. Awaiting the first casualties were 600 beds and ninety-two nurses.

Northern General was the UK's largest special surgical hospital for orthopaedics, performing nerve suture, or 'stitching', procedures as well as large-scale bone grafting. Paraffin baths were first used at Beckett's Park as preparation for massage and electric treatment. Electroshock therapy was also administered to assist post-surgical nerve regrowth as well as the retraining of muscles. Surgeons and doctors from all over the country came to observe this treatment and be educated.

Beckett's Park pioneered occupational therapy with its Curative Workshop, one of the key foundations of the treatment of disabled servicemen. The aim, of course, was to train disabled men to adapt to and support themselves in civilian and domestic life. There were classes on splint making, basket making, weaving, blacksmith's work, tailoring, shorthand and typing, shoe making, and needlecraft.

The Grand Duchess George of Russia opened the YMCA recreation hall on campus in 1915, complete with cinema equipment and facilities for concerts, lectures, plays and billiards. In March 1916 temporary huts were erected as a 700-bed annexe. However, it was apparently not all patient care and recuperation. James Graham, Director of Education for Leeds, was appalled by women students 'disporting themselves in unseemly ways' while soldiers were often to be seen thronging the tennis courts to watch the women playing.

The Odeon and the Beatles

The Beatles played the Odeon three times: June and November 1963, and 22 October 1964. On 28 June they performed at Leeds Queen's Hall. The October concert was the eleventh date of the Beatles' 1964 British tour and their final visit to Leeds' Odeon cinema. They performed two sets, for which they were paid £850. Their set comprised ten songs: 'Twist and Shout', 'Money (That's What I Want)', 'Can't Buy Me Love', 'Things We Said Today', 'I'm Happy Just To Dance With You', 'I Should Have Known Better', 'If I Fell', 'I Wanna Be Your Man', 'A Hard Day's Night' and 'Long Tall Sally'.

The Beatles live at Leeds tonight – twice!

P

The Nicola Adams Postbox

Royal Mail made a wonderful gesture to celebrate 2012 Olympic gold medal winners from Leeds with post boxes. Nicola Adams won gold in the women's flyweight boxing.

The 'Prophet Hen of Leeds'

Forty-one-year-old Mary Bateman, 'the Yorkshire Witch', was executed at York on 20 March 1809. She had been convicted of poisoning Rebecca Perigo. Mary was a farmer's daughter from Aisenby, near Thirsk. She had a lifelong history of criminal activity, stretching back to the petty theft in her childhood, and latterly took to conning people with her self- proclaimed supernatural powers and healing abilities. She married and had four children and soon became a notorious fortune teller at her home in Marsh Lane in Leeds, but her biggest claim to fame was the 'Prophet Hen of Leeds' scam in 1806. People were led to believe that the end of the world had arrived when a hen began laying eggs with 'Christ is coming' written on each one, neatly solving the old chicken and egg conundrum. Mary Bateman had written on the eggs using acid, and reinserted them into the hen's oviduct.

Rumour had it that Mary poisoned three people in 1803, although she was never tried or convicted. Her victims were two Quaker sisters and their mother who lived above their draper's shop in St Peter's Square, Quarry Hill, Leeds. Mary sold them poison potions masquerading as medicines. Having killed them, she robbed the house and shop, telling neighbours that the three women had died from plague. There was little suspicion surrounding the cause of death and no inquest.

Duplicitous as ever, Mary frequently called on the services of a 'Mrs Moore' to assist her in her scams. This fictitious lady was the source of all Mary's 'wisdom' and was always consulted on behalf of Mary's clients, who were led to believe their payments went to Mrs Moore. In 1806 Mary enlisted a new alter ego called 'Mrs Blythe'.

In 1806, a vulnerable, childless, middle-aged and reasonably well-off couple, William and Rebecca Perigo, from Bramley approached Mary seeking her help. The Perigos were not helped by their doctor, Dr Curzley, who concluded that the fluttering Rebecca experienced in her chest – probably atrial fibrillation – and her associated

Mrs Bateman mixes the poison. (From *Witchcraft, Murder, Sorcery: The Wonderful Life and Remarkable Trial of Mary Bateman of Leeds*, 1809)

psychological issues, where she claimed hauntings by a black dog and other spirits, indicated that she was under a spell and that he could do no more for her.

Mary saw this as an opportunity: she would swindle the Perigos of their money before killing them. A meeting was fixed outside at, ironically, the Black Dog pub, at which Mary requested an item of Rebecca's underclothing to send to Mrs Blythe in Scarborough – a flannel petticoat was duly 'sent off'. Mrs Blythe responded helpfully. Money changed hands and horseshoes were nailed to the Perigos' front door. Instructions were given to sew purses, supposedly containing guinea notes and gold coins, into Rebecca's bedspread and to send Mrs Blythe a cheese followed by china and silverware and some tea and sugar. A bed and bedclothes were next because Mrs Blythe could not sleep in her own bed due to the nocturnal battles she was having with Rebecca's demons.

Mary then delivered her coup de grâce, instructing Rebecca to bring her half a pound of honey, which she would mix into some of Mrs Blythe's special medicine. In addition, the Perigos were to eat puddings for six days, into each of which they were to mix a powder that Mary would give them. All correspondence and leftover pudding was to be destroyed and, if it made them ill, no doctor was to be called as Mary's treatment went beyond conventional medicine. Rebecca regularly ate her pudding, but William rarely did. Consequently, Rebecca died in May 1806 and although William reported to a doctor that he thought poison was involved in Rebecca's death, no post-mortem was ever carried out. William Perigo continued to pay Mary for another two years until he became suspicious and checked out the purses sewn into the bedclothes: the guinea notes and gold turned out to be cabbage leaves and copper. He went to the police, who arrested Mary at an entrapment meeting, to which Mary brought a bottle of arsenic and oatmeal, intending to silence William for good.

Bateman protested her innocence, but poison and personal belongings of her victims, including the Perigo couple, were found at her house. She was committed for trial at the Yorkshire Lent Assizes of 1809, which opened at York Castle on 17 March before judge Sir Simon Le Blanc. Mrs Blythe was nowhere to be found, and forensic evidence offered by a Mr Chorley found that the remains of the honey contained highly toxic mercuric chloride.

Mary attempted to avoid execution by 'pleading her belly', claiming that she was pregnant, but this was easily and swiftly disproved. Bateman was found guilty of fraud and murder and sentenced to death by hanging, to be dissected the following day. She continued to deny the murder and was finally hanged alongside two men on 20 March 1809, dying 'with a lie on her lips'. The hangman was William 'Mutton' Curry. After execution, her body was put on public display; thousands paid 3*d* to gawp at the corpse with proceeds (£30) going to charity. Some superstitious people believed that she might be saved from death by some divine intervention at the last minute. There was also a healthy trade in strips of her skin, which were sold as charms to ward off evil. After medical school dissection at Leeds Royal Infirmary, Bateman's skeleton was used in anatomy classes and, later, along with a plaster-cast death mask of her skull, was put on display on display at the Thackray Museum in Leeds until 2015, when it was returned to Leeds University Medical School.

The Pud School

There is a cookery (domestic science) class at the Leeds School of Cookery and Domestic Economy in Albion Street known as the 'Pud School'. The school was founded by the Yorkshire Ladies Council of Education in 1874 and was taken over in 1907 by the Leeds Education Committee and became part of the Yorkshire Training College of Housecraft, moving to Vernon Road in 1933. It is now part of Leeds Beckett University. The other images show children working hard with their teachers: children standing to attention in lines for an assembly in the central hall at Darley Street School, with teachers at the back, and an infant class there.

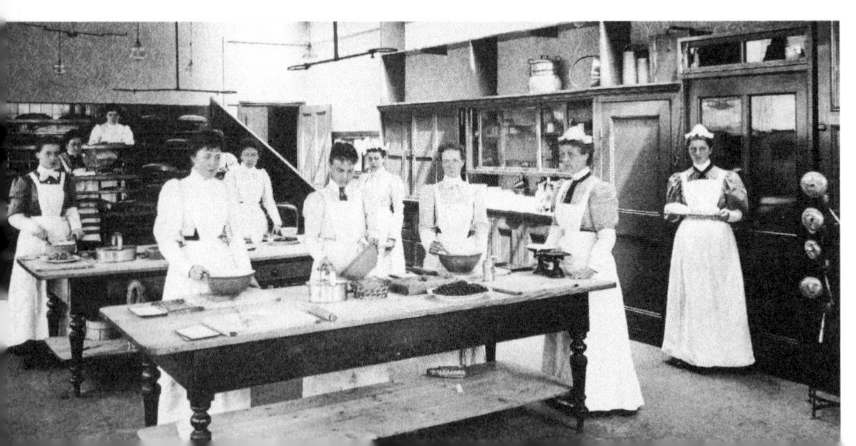

The Pud School at the Leeds School of Cookery and Domestic Economy. (Courtesy of Leodis; © Leeds Library & Information Services)

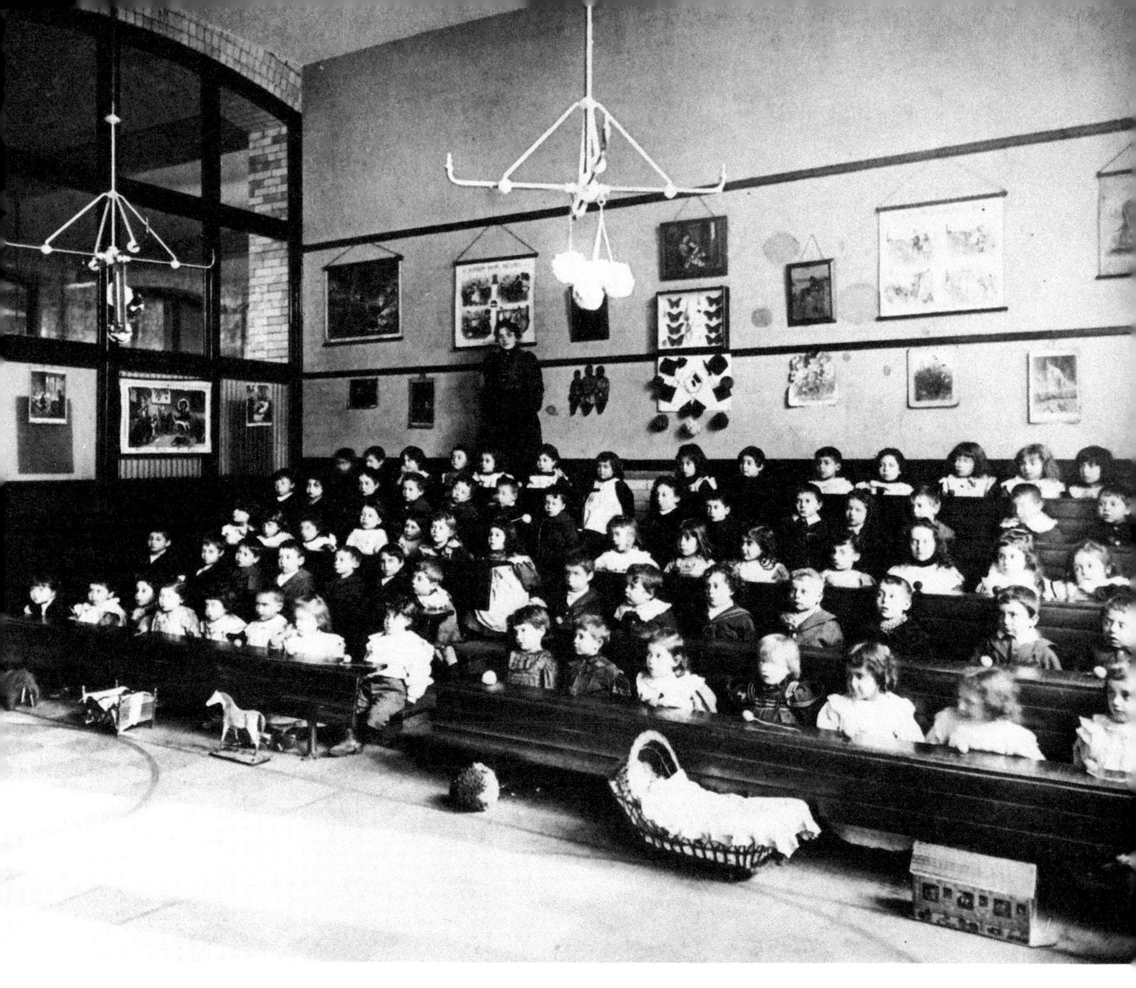

Above: Children paying attention and working hard at Darley Street School, with the teacher lurking at the back. (© Leeds Library & Information Services)

Right: Children standing to attention in lines for an assembly in the central hall at Darley Street School, with more teachers in control at the back. (Courtesy of Leodis; © Leeds Library & Information Services)

Quarry Hill

Between 1938 and 1978 Quarry Hill was the biggest social housing complex in the United Kingdom. Its design owed much to such modernist developments as the Karl Marx-Hof in Vienna, and La Cité de la Muette in Paris. The homes at Quarry Hill could boast modern features such as solid fuel ranges, electric lighting, a state-of-the-art (but inefficient) refuse Garchey disposal system and communal facilities.

The original plan for Quarry Hill was for 800 flats, which increased to 938. In addition, there was a community hall with seating for 520 people, including a stage and dressing rooms (never built), twenty shops (few opened), indoor and outdoor swimming pools, a paddling pool, courtyards and gardens. There was to be an estate nursery, playgrounds, lawns and recreation areas, a communal laundry with dryers (drying of clothes on the balconies was prohibited, all washing and drying was to be done here), and, to end it all, an estate mortuary. Eighty-eight two-person passenger lifts were fitted.

Quarry House was built on the site of the former Quarry Hill Flats at Quarry Hill. It houses the regional offices of the Department of Health and the Department for

Above left: The completed Quarry Hill complex ... well, nearly.

Above right: Quarry Hill under construction. (Courtesy of Leodis. © Leeds Library & Information Services)

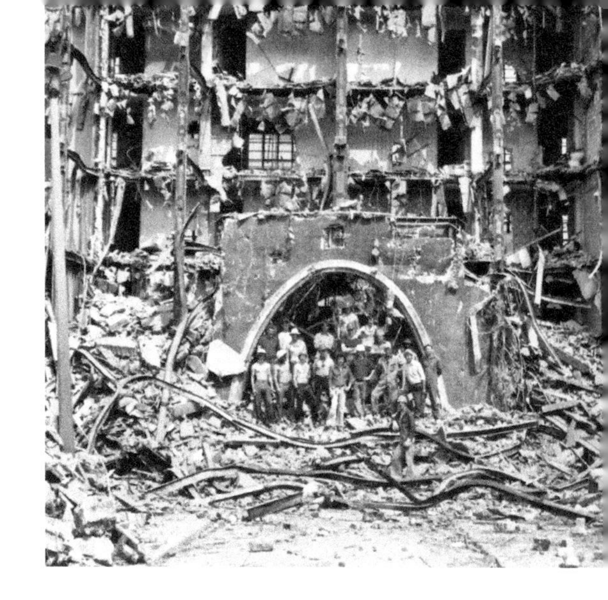

Demolition in full swing in 1978 on a card entitled 'Noel and His Lads'. This was the last standing arch at Quarry Hill. (© Peter Mitchell)

Work and Pensions. This powerful-looking building has earned itself the nicknames 'The Kremlin' (photography is verboten) and 'The Ministry of Truth' after Orwell's *Nineteen Eighty-Four.*

It cost £ 55 million and keeps over 2,000 civil servants busy. When they are not as busy they can partake of the facilities at the Forum leisure centre: swimming pool, a sports hall, squash courts and a fitness room 'fully equipped with the latest Polaris cardio-vascular, static-resistant and free-weight equipment', where civil servants can work out while watching TV. However, it is by no means cheap and costs employees over £300 per year. The Woodpecker pub, however, serves (tax payer) subsidised beer. Over £500,000 was spent on 'decorating' the building, under a government scheme requiring that 1 per cent of the cost of their new buildings be spent on art. Sadly, the people of Leeds do not see or enjoy any of this.

Above: Slum conditions, which were prevalent throughout Leeds. It was this that the Quarry Hill development was intended to put an end to. (Courtesy of Leodis. © Leeds Library & Information Services)

Right: The Quarry House.

Dorothy Una Ratcliffe (1887–1967)

In the Leeds City Museum there is a serene but powerful bronze of a woman reading. It is Dorothy Una Ratcliffe, niece of Lord Brotherton and writer of poetry in Yorkshire dialect.

She is one of the celebrated (but often overlooked) women poets of the First World War. An example of her work is 'Julian Hunter, Soldier Poet – An Idyll in the Dales' (Collected in L. London, *Female Poets of the First World War*, Volume 2, 2016). She helped Lord Brotherton equip the Leeds Old Pals Regiment. A fluent French speaker, she also assisted with settling Leeds's quota of Belgian refugees.

Dorothy Una Ratcliffe (often known simply as DUR) was a flamboyant, colourful and bohemian woman. She published forty-nine books, travelled the world, tended her garden, loved Yorkshire and its traditions, was a prolific collector and inspired a magnificent legacy to the city of Leeds. She was raised in Sussex and Surrey, the eldest of the three daughters of George Benson Clough, a rich barrister from Scarborough – she called him the first Yorkshireman in her life. The author of several books himself, he encouraged her early literary efforts.

In London in 1909, aged twenty-two, she married Charles Frederick Ratcliffe, nephew and heir of the Leeds chemical tycoon Edward Allen Brotherton, later Lord Brotherton of

The serene but powerful bronze of Dorothy Una Ratcliffe in the Leeds City Museum.

Wakefield, a childless widower. The newly married couple settled in a house near Edward Brotherton's home at Roundhay Hall (later the Spire Hospital), and eventually moved in to the hall themselves. Brotherton and Ratcliffe shared a love for literature and fine books. He underwrote her literary magazine, *The Microcosm*, which featured articles by writers like Tolkien and Chesterton. She helped him build up a magnificent library of rare and precious books and manuscripts, later bequeathed to Leeds University 'in trust for the Nation', and now housed in the Brotherton Library, which he had endowed.

Ratcliffe developed a deep love for the Yorkshire Dales – their landscape, dialect and traditions – and in 1918 published her first volume of lyrical, romantic Dales ballads *The Dales of Arcady* (after Keats's *Ode on a Grecian Urn*) followed year after year with poems, plays and memoirs, all based on Dales life – some in local dialect and some for children. Poems include 'White Dog of Yockenthwaite', 'Mad Old Mike', 'Croodle Beck' and 'April in Wensleydale'. Her near obsession with the Romanies and their culture led to works on gypsy life written in what she termed the 'old ballad tradition'. Her gypsy poems 'Brough Hill Fair' and 'Yorkshire Gypsy' are examples. In the 1920s, with her marriage to wayward Charles on the rocks and determined not to divorce lest the scandal damage Lord Brotherton's political career, Dorothy bought a small country house, Laverton Grange, in Kirby Malzeard, near Ripon, from where she could explore the Dales at will.

Ratcliffe was always an active supporter of the Yorkshire dialect and gypsy lore societies, and remained faithful to the Brotherton Library, to which she donated her collection of Romany material. The Leeds Museum holds her collection of fans and miniatures, and, sadly, baby bonnets – she was unable to bear children thanks to complications from a so-called cure for a sexually transmitted infection caught from her first husband.

Romulus and Remus

The City Museum is home to the wonderful Roman mosaic depicting the legendary she-wolf Lupa suckling Romulus and Remus, founders of Rome. It dates from around CE 250 and was discovered at Aldborough (Isurium Brigantum, www.leedsmuseum.co.uk)

The mosaic of Lupa at the City Museum.

Royal Armouries Museum, Clarence Dock

The Royal Armouries Museum displays the national collection of arms and armour and is the National Fireams Centre. It is part of the Royal Armouries family of three museums, the others being the Tower of London and Fort Nelson, near Portsmouth.

Interestingly, the museum was designed from the inside out. The design took the display spaces, together with the study collections, conservation workshops and library as the foundation of its overall layout. The ceiling heights were specifically made so that the longest weapons in the collections, displayed vertically, and the principal lift needed to move the largest object, could be accommodated comfortably.

Five galleries house 75,000 objects along with the Peace Gallery. The museum also features the Hall of Steel, a huge staircase 'whose walls are decorated with trophy displays composed of 2,500 objects reminiscent of the historical trophy displays erected by the Tower Armouries from the 17th century'. The galleries are War, Hunting, Oriental, Tournament and Self-defence.

Above left: Armed Indian war elephant.

Above right: The Hall of Steel.

Left: English armour of the seventeenth century.

S

The Savage Club

Edmund Bogg, writer, rambler and bohemian, founded the Leeds Savage Club around 1891. When 'T'owd Chief' was not busy rambling or travelling around Yorkshire, armed to the teeth with sketch pads, pencils and notebooks rather than bows and arrows, he was hard at work penning one of his many excellent books on his beloved Yorkshire countryside, books for which he is still justly remembered today.

Bogg came from the Wolds hamlet of Duggleby where his father was a wheelwright. Schooling was in short supply as was, presumably, action of any sort and so when he was twenty he went to Leeds in search of work, which he found in joinery and then as a 'colourman', mixing paints for artists. The bohemian artists he met appealed and he, combining both of his new skills, set up in business as a picture dealer and framer with a gallery and workshop in Woodhouse Lane, living nearby with his wife Fanny and their young family. In due course he attracted a coterie of young artists (including Owen Bowen) whom he paid to go off to paint in the countryside and bring back to Leeds artworks he could sell in his shop.

Leeds Savage Club, modelled on the Savage Club in London (founded in 1857 and still one of the leading Bohemian Gentleman's Clubs in London) brought together Leeds artists, musicians and writers into a refuge from the restrictions of the everyday world. Membership was restricted to only fifty members, who were called 'Savages', with a 'Chief' as president, a 'Scribe' as secretary and Braves as committee men. The American Indian theme was Edmund Bogg's idea and he was duly elected 'Chief', presiding in feathers and warpaint over the usually boisterous pow-wows in the 'Wigwam', fuelled by firewater (whisky punch).

For Bogg, books came next. In 1892 he published *A Thousand Miles in Wharfedale and the Basin of the Wharfe* in which he describes a journey accompanied by his artist friends, full of florid descriptions of village and countryside, historical snippets and wonderful illustrations courtesy of fellow travellers like Percy Robinson and Gilbert Foster, along with his own photographs. Its success led to *Edenvale to the Plain of York Or, a Thousand Miles in the Valleys of the Nidd and Yore* followed by *A Thousand Miles of Wandering Along the Roman Wall, the Old Border Region, Lakeland, and Ribblesdale*, *Richmondshire And The Vale Of Mowbray*, *The Charm*

Of The Hambletons Round About Thirsk, Coxwold, Kilburn,Byland And Rievaulx and in 1902 the bestseller *Old Kingdom of Elmet*, which includes a description of Leeds around the turn of the twentieth century.

Bogg died at his home in Caledonian Road, Leeds, aged eighty-one. Characteristically, he wrote his own epitaph: 'Bid adieu to the hills and vales, rivers and glens [and] glide gently down the river of life to journey's end, like the beautiful Wharfe.'

Jogendra Sen

Jogendra Sen was a highly educated, multilingual Bengali who graduated in electrical engineering at the University of Leeds in 1913. He was one of the first to sign up to the 1st Leeds 'Pals' Battalion in September 1914. Jogendra remains the only known non-white soldier to serve with the 15th West Yorkshire Regiment during the war. Despite his education and intellect, he was rejected as an officer (we can probably guess why) and did not progress beyond the rank of private.

Jogendra was killed in action at Bus-lès-Artois in the Somme department. He was part of a wiring party that was bombarded late on the night of 22 May 1916. After being hit by shrapnel in the leg and neck, the Bengali succumbed to his wounds. Private Sen's name can be seen on the university's war memorial in the Brotherton Library entrance hall.

In total, India contributed some 1.5 million men as soldiers and non-combatants, including labourers and porters, to the war. Dr Santanu Das, reader in English at King's College London and an expert on India's involvement in the First World War, paid a visit in 2005 to Sen's home town of Chandernagore – a former French colony. There Dr Das saw Sen's bloodstained glasses in a display case in the town's museum, the Institut de Chandernagore. He said: 'I was absolutely stunned when I saw the pair of glasses. It's one of the most poignant artefacts I've seen – a mute witness to the final moments of Sen's life. It was astonishing that something so fragile has survived when almost everything else has perished.'

Professor Arthur Smithell

The British aniline dye industry was seriously impaired by the outbreak of war. By February 1915 there remained a mere three months' supply of dyes left in the United Kingdom. Aniline dyes were essential in both civilian and military clothing production. To make matters even worse, coal tar, from which aniline dyes are derived, was hijacked for use in the manufacture of the explosive tri-nitrotoluene (TNT). Professor Arthur Green was Chair of Tinctorial (Colour) Chemistry at the University of Leeds from 1903 to 1916 and one of the chemists in a committee tasked with solving the problems of chemical supplies required for dyes and explosives. The committee established British Dyes Ltd to alleviate the aniline dye shortage. Green then focused on increasing explosives production, developing better ways of making picric acid, a key component in explosives, also useful as an antiseptic and for burns treatment. Green's sterling work at Leeds was continued by Arthur Perkin.

Professor of Chemistry Arthur Smithells' main contribution was instructing troops in gas warfare. He served as a visiting lecturer to the camps of the Northern Command and later as chief chemical adviser for anti-gas training of the Home Forces, attaining the honorary rank of lieutenant-colonel. Smithells proceeded to demystify the science underpinning gas warfare by educating the troops in effective responses to its use, banishing what he termed the scientific and chemical 'illiteracy', and promulgating an understanding of the basic chemical principles involved. Smithell debunked many of the myths surrounding war gas, not least the instinctive reaction of the soldier to flee or seek refuge at the bottom of a trench, whereas in reality it was those who stayed at their posts rather than those who ran away, and those who remained on the fire step rather than at the bottom of the trench where the gas was at is densest, who suffered least.

Temple Works, Holbeck Urban Village

A Grade I listed Victorian former flax mill that has gone down in history as containing the largest room in the world, with sheep grazing on a sky-lit roof amid an industrially revolutionised Leeds. Temple Works, or Temple Mill, comprised an office block and factory, the former being based on the temple at Antaeopolis and Temple of Horus at Edfu with a chimney in the shape of an obelisk. The factory building was modelled on the Typhonium at Dendera.

Benjamin Hick's 240-hp beam engine featured Egyptian details, including a regulator in the form of a winged solar disk. The Egyptian influence came from Marshall's intense interest in Egyptology. The sheep were not just a gimmick; they helped retain humidity in the flax mill to prevent the linen thread from becoming dried out and unworkable. Sheep, of course, are not very good at climbing ladders or stairs, so to get them onto the roof and down again the hydraulic lift had to be invented, and so it was.

To this day it is referred to in schools of architecture and engineering the world over not just for the breathtaking façade but also for the unique and visionary engineering solution used for the main mill floor, reminiscent of Frank Lloyd Wright's Johnson Wax Building completed 100 years later in Racine, Wisconsin. Up until 1981 it was the northern headquarters of the mail-order catalogue company Kay's from 1953 until its closure in 1981 when they moved to a four-storey warehouse in Sweet Street. Kay's was the largest employer in south Leeds.

Edfu.

Above left and right: The magnificent Temple Works today.

From 2009 'Temple.Works.Leeds' has been a thriving cultural hub that is given over to 20 per cent heritage and education, 40 per cent location shoots and in-house studio events, and 40 per cent public events.

In 1842 there was trouble at the mill with the Plug Plot Riots (the 1842 General Strike). They got the name 'Plug' because the mills 'were stopped from working by the removal or "drawing" of a few bolts or "plugs" in the boilers so as to prevent steam from being raised' (OED). The Leeds Annals described the events:

> Mr J. G. Marshall was one of the pioneers of workers' safety and education and did much to mitigate the dangers inherent in running and working in a textile mill. He was only too aware of the flammability of textiles and so built twenty-five fire escapes into his building; multi-storey spelled death trap with carnage and mayhem a possibility on stairways so he made temple Works single storey. Like Rowntree, Titus Salt and Cadbury he felt a social responsibility towards his workers and their families: the undercroft housed children's dormitories, shops, doctors, a church; there was a school adjacent to the mill at ground level. The children, until aged twelve, were well looked after while their parents worked to bring home the bacon.

Thackray Museum, Beckett Street

The building now housing the fascinating Thackray Medical Museum opened in 1861 as the first purpose-built Leeds Union Workhouse, accommodating 784 paupers. Over time new buildings were added to the workhouse, including a separate infirmary. By the end of the nineteenth century the buildings were mainly used for medical care of the poor rather than traditional workhouse activity, the reason being that Leeds initially opted not to cooperate with the New Poor Law. Its Local Act status exempted it from many of the provisions of the 1834 Poor Law Amendment Act. However, in 1844, the Poor Law Commissioners placed the township's poor relief administration under a new body – the Leeds Guardians. One of the first things they did was build, in 1848, the Moral and Industrial Training Schools on the north side of Beckett Street in Leeds.

Above left: Moving and growing activity zone in the Thackray Medical Museum, Leeds. Entrance to feature on the digestive system. (By Chemical Engineer)

Above right: Part of a street showing various activities of the time from shops to privies and information about specific people who once lived there, and their medical afflictions, treatments and death. (By Chemical Engineer)

During the First World War it was called the East Leeds War Hospital, caring for armed services personnel. In 1925 the Leeds Union Workhouse infirmary was repurposed and renamed St James's Hospital. In 1945, the rest of the workhouse had merged with the hospital and it became part of the NHS in 1948. By the 1990s, the old Leeds Union Workhouse building was considered unfit for the practice of modern medicine. Permission was then given for it to house the Thackray Medical Museum, which opened in 1997.

Features include 'Leeds 1842: Life in Victorian Leeds', a walk through slum streets with authentic sights, sounds and smells, and following the lives, illnesses and treatments of eight Victorians, making choices that determine their survival, or otherwise, among the rats, fleas and bugs.

Amputation tools from 1870. (By Chemical Engineer)

Part of the Wilkinson Apothecary Gallery. A display of apothecary ceramic ware. (By Chemical Engineer)

'Pain, Pus and Blood' describes surgery before anaesthesia and advances in pain relief, and 'Having a Baby' focuses on developments in childbirth safety.

Hannah Dyson's 'Ordeal' is a video reconstruction of 1842 surgery, pre-anaesthetics. You watch as a surgeon, his assistant and a group of trainee doctors prepare for Hannah Dyson's operation – the amputation of her leg crushed in a mill accident. (The actual operation is not seen.)

'The Life Zone' is an interactive children's gallery looking at how the human body works, with a smaller room for under-fives. The museum was, as noted, also home of the skeleton of Mary Bateman, the 'Yorkshire Witch', who was executed for fraud and murder in 1809.

Ralph Thoresby

Ralph Thoresby, the North's answer to Samuel Pepys, kept a diary and published, among other works, his famous *Ducatus Leodiensis*, the first history of Leeds. The city's historical society, formed in 1889, was named after him. By the early eighteenth-century Leeds was largely a mercantile town. The population exploded from 10,000 at the end of the seventeenth century to 30,000 at the end of the eighteenth. In the 1770s Leeds merchants contributed 30 per cent of the country's woollen exports, valued at £1,500,000. Seventy years previously the whole of Yorkshire accounted for only 20 per cent of the nation's exports.

Thoresby established the first covered cloth market. This was the White Cloth Hall, which opened in 1711 behind the Corn Exchange, and traded here for sixty-five years before moving to the Calls. In 1758 the Coloured Cloth Hall, or Mixed Cloth Hall, was built near Mill Hill for the sale of dyed cloth, capacious enough for 1800 trading stalls,

The third White Cloth Hall today.

initially let at 3 guineas per annum, but later trading at a premium of £24 per annum. The hall was demolished in 1899 to make way for the new General Post Office. The last White Cloth Hall met its end in 1896 to allow for the Metropole Hotel.

Thornton's Arcade, off Briggate

The buildings and conditions in what would become the beautiful Victoria Quarter could not have been more different before 1877. Vicar Lane was full of slaughterhouses, butchers, fruit and vegetable stalls.

That was before the famous theatre architect Frank Matcham was commissioned to redevelop the area. Matcham could, by then, put his name to more than 200 theatres and music halls, including the London Palladium and Coliseum. For the new Victoria Arcade he used opulent marbles, gilded mosaics, imposing cast and wrought iron, as well as carved and polished mahogany, to create two streets, an arcade and the Empire Theatre – this was demolished in the 1960s and Harvey Nichols now occupies the site.

Highlights (literally) are Brian Clarke's breathtaking stained-glass roof, extending the full length of Queen Victoria Street, and the largest stained-glass window in Britain – 746.9 square metres. There are also three splendid mosaic floor panels by

Above left: Thornton's Arcade – showing the spectacular roof.

Above right: The brilliant and beautiful Ivanhoe Clock, made by the famous Leeds clockmakers Potts & Sons, at the west end of the arcade. The painted, almost lifesize, figures are all from Sir Walter Scott's *Ivanhoe*. Left to right, they are Robin Hood in green, Friar Tuck in black, Richard the Lionheart in red, and Gurth the Swineherd in khaki. They have moving parts, each one helping to strike the quarter or the hours.

Right: More unalloyed magnificence.

Joanna Veevers in County Arcade. The original ornate mahogany frames survived the dilapidation and the gilded art nouveau lettering has been restored.

Thornton's three-storey arcade was the first to open in 1878 named after Charles Thornton. The arcade is famous for its clock, made by William Potts & Sons of Leeds, which features animated life-sized characters from Sir Walter Scott's *Ivanhoe*. Robin Hood and Gurth the Swineherd strike the quarter hours; Friar Tuck and Richard the Lionheart strike the hours. At the other end of the arcade is a woman's head, sporting long curling hair and a large hat. She is modelled on Gainsborough's portrait of the Duchess of Devonshire.

Charles Thornton (1820–81) owned the Old White Swan Inn in Swan Street and was the proprietor of the Varieties Music Hall (now the Leeds City Varieties). In 1873 he built a block of shops and offices, Thornton's Buildings, where the Upper Headrow meets with Lands Lane. In 1875 Thornton sought permission to demolish the Old Talbot Inn on Briggate to build a new arcade of shops on the site. The Talbot was not just any old pub, it was one of the oldest inns in Leeds and boasted frescoes on the walls of a room there. The inn was a venue for cockfighting, and in the seveneenth century it was where the circuit judge stayed while in Leeds.

Time Ball Buildings, Nos 24–26 Briggate (*c.* 1820)

A precious and rare surviving example of elaborate and ornate Victorian-Edwardian shop innovation and design. The premises had a number of occupants over the years:

Time Ball Buildings.

distiller, saddler and trunk maker, a barber and perfumier, and a stationer through the nineteenth century until 1871 when Boar Lane was being rebuilt and the premises were empty. In 1872 J. Dyson, watchmaker, was at No. 26 and by 1872 occupied the whole building.

Most of the elaborate façade was added by Dyson. Bay windows flank the large pedimented clock case at Nos 25 and 26. At No. 24, Father Time surmounts a large framed clock on the third storey. There are ironwork spandrels, the letters 'D & S', and the Latin words *'Tempus Fugit'*. Gold lettering shows the date as '1865'. The stunning gilded time ball mechanism was linked to Greenwich and dropped at precisely 1 p.m. each day. This feature, together with the window mechanism, which raised and lowered the window displays, allowing safe storage in the vaults each night, makes Dyson's unique.

J. R. R. Tolkien

J. R. R. Tolkien came to Leeds in 1920 with his wife Edith and small sons to take up the post of Reader in English Language at the university. The Thoresby Society website continues the story: 'They settled in a small terrace house, 11 St Mark's Terrace, near the University. It was dingy and dark, and the sooty air rotted the curtains and covered the baby outside in his pram with smuts! In 1924, with a third child on the way, they moved to greener, pleasanter surroundings at 2 Darnley Road, West Park, Headingley, a tall Edwardian red-brick semi next to fields.'

The Tolkiens lived in St Michael's Road, in between St Mark's and Darnley Road, before moving to Holly Bank – both in Headingley.

Tolkien's academic work at Leeds reveals an interest in local dialect influenced by his Yorkshire environment and landscapes. As a member of the Yorkshire Dialect Society he wrote the foreword to Walter E. Haigh's *New Glossary of the Dialect of the Huddersfield District.* Here he mentions his influential 1925 edition of *Sir Gawain and the Green Knight* (edited with E. V. Gordon) in which 'Tolkien ... was charmed by the way in which words familiar to him only from the medieval poem reappeared in modern dialect speech. He gives more than a dozen examples, including the dialect verb "dloppen" in Huddersfield "to frighten, surprise, amaze, disgust".' In *Sir Gawain* it is a verb with an identical meaning.

In 1925 Tolkien returned to Oxford to take up the post of Professor of Anglo-Saxon Studies, which, along with his Merton Professorship of English Language and Literature from 1945 to 1959 and his writing, kept him busy for the rest of his working life.

Tomasso Bros, Ice-cream Supremos

Tomasso Bris – kings of Leeds ice cream.

A delivery van for Sharp's basket and skep manufacturers.

The Boston poulterers.

University of Leeds Brotherton Library, Parkinson Building

The Brotherton Library is a Grade II listed beaux arts building with art deco fittings completed in 1936 and is named after Edward Brotherton, who bequeathed

The Brotherton Library, based on – but bigger than – the old reading room at the British Library in the British Museum.

£100,000 as funding for the University of Leeds' first purpose-built library in 1927. In the beginning, while the university was still Leeds College, it stocked all of the university's books and manuscripts, except the books housed in the separate Medical Library and Clothworkers' Textile Library. Nowadays, it provides the home for the collections in arts, social sciences and law, and various special collections, archives and gallery.

The first library here dates from 1894 and was in the undercroft of College Hall, part of the Yorkshire College, originally founded as the Leeds School of Medicine in 1831. The college became part of the Victoria University in 1887. Fanny Passavant was the first librarian, who retired in 1919 when the library, bursting at the seams, contained 65,000 volumes. The façade of the Parkinson building is of Portland stone, but the exterior of the Brotherton Library is plain red brick. This is because access was to be through the Parkinson Building, so there was no need to have a Portland stone exterior when the library was obscured. However, lack of funding delayed the completion of the Parkinson so the Brotherton's bland exterior was visible for fourteen years.

There is absolutely nothing bland about the splendid interior. It is modelled on the old reading room at the British Museum, although, with a diameter of 160 feet, it is deliberately wider than the 140 feet of the British Museum's reading room. Twenty columns of green Swedish marble, each comprising three 3-ton drums, support the coffered dome. The surrounding balcony has an ornate iron balustrade, and an art deco electrolier hangs from the dome's centre.

Treasures include locks of hair from the heads of Mozart and Beethoven; Shakespeare's First Folio, Newton's *Philosophiæ Naturalis Principia Mathematica* (1687) and Oscar Wilde's *The Duchess of Padua* (1883).

Above left: Swedish marble abounds.

Above right: The art deco electrolier.

V

Victoria Cross

Alfred Atkinson VC (6 February 1874 to 21 February 1900) came from Armley. His father, James Harland Atkinson, was a farrier in the Royal Artillery. Alfred was twenty-six years old when he died, and a sergeant in the 1st Battalion, The Princess of Wales's Own (Yorkshire Regiment). His valiant action took place on 18 February 1900 during the Battle of Paardeberg, for which he was posthumously awarded the VC:

> No. 3264 Sergeant A. Atkinson, Yorkshire Regiment.
> During the battle of Paardeburg, 18th February, 1900, Sergeant A. Atkinson, 1st Battalion Yorkshire Regiment, went out seven times, under heavy and close fire, to obtain water for the wounded. At the seventh attempt he was wounded in the head, and died a few days afterwards.

His Victoria Cross can be seen at the Green Howards Museum, Richmond.

Explosion of an ammunition wagon during the Battle of Paardeberg, Boer War. (Courtesy of New York Public Library Photography Collection)

John Waddington

When we think of the Leeds firm Waddingtons images of ‘Monopoly’ and ‘Cluedo’ spring to mind. But Waddingtons had a far more diverse range of products than the iconic board game and decks of cards might suggest.

Who's the murderer? Every player a detective! The game that's different!
'CLUEDO'—THE GREAT DETECTIVE GAME
Games... more popular for Christmas than ever... and the great thriller game 'CLUEDO' will be the favourite!
WHY CRIME DETECTION FASCINATES so many people nobody knows, but it does! 'CLUEDO' is a game of skill completely different from any other game. The winner is the detective who, by sheer detection, discovers the murderer, the place of the crime, and the instrument used by the murderer.
For 2 to 6 players, and a delight for the whole family. The game that's so different! Price 25/-
Give games and delight the whole family
Make your Christmas gift selection from
WADDINGTON'S GAMES
at all stationers and stores

TOTOPOLY
25/-
'TOTOPOLY'—Horse-training and racing game.
21/-
'MONOPOLY' — The real estate game.

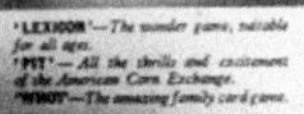

PIT
2/6
8/6
5/-
'LEXICON'—The wonder game, suitable for all ages.
'PIT'—All the thrills and excitement of the American Corn Exchange.
'WHOT'—The amazing family card game.

5/9
WADDINGTON'S—The only Circular Jig Saw Puzzles. Over 500 pieces; fully interlocking; and handsomely boxed. Many other Series—3/-, 3/-, 5/4 each.

A 1952 advert for Cluedo – those were the days.

The First World War saw a boom in the demand for playing cards, which Waddingtons helped to meet. In 1941, the British Secret Service (MI9) commissioned the company to produce a special edition of 'Monopoly' for prisoners of war held by the Germans. Secreted inside these sets were maps, compasses, real foreign currency and other objects essential for a successful escape. The games were distributed to camp escape committees by the International Red Cross. The escape and evasion maps, which also went in decks of playing cards, were printed on Bemberg silk (rayon) or on mulberry paper. Churchill himself encouraged an increase in production of cards to boost morale at home and abroad. The company also produced cartridge casings for ICI metals.

Keith Waterhouse (1929–2009)

Keith Waterhouse was born in industrial Hunslet, Leeds. He is best known for his novel *Billy Liar* (1959) and the subsequent John Schlesinger film featuring Hull-born actor Tom Courtenay in the part of Billy.

Waterhouse's career started at the *Yorkshire Evening Post*, but he was also a regular writer for *Punch*, the *Daily Mirror*, and the *Daily Mail*. In his early days he campaigned against the colour bar in post-war Britain, the abuses committed by the British in Kenya, and the British government's selling weapons to various Middle Eastern countries.

Above: Industrial Leeds, 1950s.

Right: *Billy Liar*: a few weeks in the life of the young boy on a council estate and in the surrounding rhubarb fields, quarries and clerk of works' yard that form his playground. (East Grove Street, Burmantofts, 1954. © Marc Riboud)

While at the *Mirror* during a newspaper strike in 1956 he wrote his first novel, *There Is A Happy Land*, set on a Leeds housing estate and which, like *Billy Liar*, draws on his boyhood in the industrial landscape of Hunslet. The book is further enriched because it is replete with Yorkshire slang and the evocation of his own experiences allows Waterhouse to vividly recreate so his half-feral street urchins.

In an interview with *The Guardian* of 14 April 2001, Waterhouse describes how his Hunslet-Leeds childhood informed his work:

> The best guess is somewhere in a working-class Leeds childhood that, Waterhouse perceptively notes, although packed with escapism, was in fact an escape into realism. He was transfixed by the nitty gritty of Leeds life, and his recollection of his adventures around the city invest the place with the same lyrical nostalgia that Woody Allen does to his childhood New York. Fellow Leeds boy Gerald Kaufman said Waterhouse's 1994 memoir, City Lights, gave back to him, "the Leeds that I loved, the Leeds that time and change had taken away".

Joseph Watson & Sons Ltd – Soapy Joe's

Joseph Watson & Sons Ltd – Soapy Joe's – had its soap factory in Whitehall Road. Unlikely as it may seem at first, this soap manufacturer largely turned its hand away from soaps (which were rationed) to the manufacture of hand grenades, rifle grenades and anti-tank grenades, bomb tail units and valve bodies for the J bomb. Glycerine, of course, was used in the production of TNT, with glycerine a by-product of the soap-making process. Joseph Watson with his expertise was called upon assist the government in the establishment of national munitions factories and in particular the No. 1 National Shell Filling Factory at Barnbow.

A Soapy Joe advert.

The White Cloth Hall, Kirkgate

Leeds, lying on the fringes of the Yorkshire cloth-producing district, had to compete for trade with better-placed neighbouring towns, so in 1711 all the cloth business was centralised in the purpose-built first White Cloth Hall on Kirkgate. Indeed, Leeds' White Cloth Hall was a direct riposte to the merchants of Wakefield, who, in an undisguised attempt to attract business away from Leeds, built a cloth hall to house their market. This was much better than the Leeds market at the time, being indoors and protected from the weather. Leeds merchants had no choice but to do the same, and a cloth hall for the trading of white (that is, undyed) cloth was built on Kirkgate on a site provided by Lord Irwin of Temple Newsam with £1,000 contributed by merchants and tradesmen. Thoresby describes it as 'built upon Pillars and Arches in the form of an Exchange, with a Quadrangular Court within'. The new White Cloth Hall was built on the site of some former almshouses. Some white cloth continued to be sold in Briggate. The White Cloth building is still there, but is somewhat dilapidated.

Predictably, perhaps, the Leeds trade soon outgrew the cloth hall and in 1755 the clothiers financed the building of the second White Cloth Hall south of the river

A poster advertising a performance of Pablo Fanque's Grand Allied Circus in Rochdale. The Leeds poster would have been very similar.

on Meadow Lane. But this second White Cloth Hall also soon proved inadequate, and, smarting at the opening of a rival cloth hall at Gomersal, in 1774 the Leeds merchants agreed on the building of a third hall in Leeds. A site was found on a piece of land called the Tenter Ground in the Calls. The new hall was built around a large central courtyard and at the northern end it was two storeys high, with assembly rooms on the upper storey. This hall opened in 1775. In 1776 the management of the cloth hall passed from the merchants to the clothiers, and a Committee of Trustees was set up to be responsible for the organisation of the cloth market. It held 1,210 merchant stalls.

It was not all hard work and endless business at the Cloth Hall. The central yard was occasionally used for spectacular events, as in 1786 when a Mr Lunardi made a 'balloon ascent from the area of the White Cloth Hall, amidst the plaudits of 30,000 people'. More famously, the White Cloth Hall Yard played host to Pablo Fanque's Grand Allied Circus, as evidenced by an 1858 poster, a similar one of which influenced John Lennon to feature the grand master on 'Being for the Benefit of Mr Kite'.

The railways intervened in 1865 when this White Cloth Hall was demolished to make way for the railway. In 1868, as compensation, the railway company built a new hall on King Street. This fourth White Cloth Hall never really got off the ground and it was demolished in 1895. The Met Hotel occupies the site today – the cupola on the hotel roof was once part of the cloth hall.

Not everyone could trade in the cloth halls. Clothiers were obliged to have served a seven-year apprenticeship first – later reduced to five years. Anyone wanting to sell cloth who did not qualify, the so-called 'Irregulars', had to use a separate building, which was first in Meadow Lane and then from 1792 on the ground floor of the Music Hall in Albion Street, which was known as 'Tom Paine's Hall'.

Not surprisingly, the mixed or coloured cloth makers who were still using the open-air market in Briggate wanted their own cloth hall. Accordingly, a patch of land in the 'Park' was bought – now the site of City Square and Infirmary Street. Each wing of

Inside the Mixed Cloth Hall.

the building was divided into two 'streets' with two rows of stands. It was used by a massive 1,770 clothiers who could buy a stand for £2 10*s*. The hall, Leeds' largest, cost £5,300 and opened in 1756. The central courtyard could hold 20,000 people. This was also used for public meetings where the steps acted as a platform for the speakers – in 1880 Gladstone addressed a Liberal Party meeting there. A small octagonal building, the 'Exchange' or 'Rotunda', was later added, used as an office by the trustees who were responsible for the running of the property. The hall was knocked down in 1890 and replaced by the post office in City Square.

The White and Mixed Cloth Halls were highly prestigious institutions and any important visitor to the city was given a guided tour to see the textile markets in operation; one such visitor in 1768 to the Mixed Cloth Hall was the King of Denmark.

Whitelocks Alehouse, Turk's Head Yard

Grade II listed, Whitelock's Alehouse first opened its doors in 1715 as the Turk's Head, fittingly enough, in Turk's Head Yard. It is Leeds' oldest surviving pub.

In 1867 John Lupton Whitelock, an accomplished flautist with the Hallé and Leeds Symphony Orchestra, was granted the licence of the Turk's Head. The Whitelock family bought the pub in the 1880s and in 1886 completed a refurbishment, which

Whitelocks – the oldest in Leeds, largely unspoilt and one of the country's best.

has left the décor we can still see today, including the long marble topped bar, etched mirrors and glass.

In the mid-1890s the pub was rebadged as Whitelock's First City Luncheon Bar and in 1897 John Lupton Whitelock installed electricity, including an exciting new revolving searchlight, at the Briggate entrance to the yard. Trick beer glasses in which a sovereign was placed ensured the punter got, not the money, but an electric shock.

John Betjeman described Whitelocks as 'the Leeds equivalent of Fleet Street's Old Cheshire Cheese and far less self-conscious, and does a roaring trade. It is the very heart of Leeds'. It figures in *Great Bars of the World* rubbing shoulders with the Long Bar in Shanghai's Peace Hotel and Harry's in Venice.

Inside Whitelocks with superb mirrors and stained glass.

Outside Whitelocks.

Prince George (1902–42), later Duke of Kent, threw a party here in a curtained-off section of the restaurant. In those days a doorman ensured that men wore dinner jackets. Women were not allowed at the bar, so waiters served drinks to the women where they sat.

The Who, *Live at Leeds*

Live at Leeds is a live album by The Who. It was recorded at the University of Leeds refectory on 14 February 1970 and is the only live album that was released while the group were still actively recording and performing in their famous line-up of Roger Daltrey, Pete Townsend, John Entwistle and Keith Moon.

Two shows were scheduled – one at the University of Leeds and the other at the University of Hull – to record and release a live album. The shows were performed on 14 February 1970 at Leeds and on 15 February at Hull, but technical problems with the recordings from the Hull concert – the bass guitar had not been recorded on some of the songs – made it inevitable that the Leeds show be released as the album. Townshend subsequently mixed the live tapes, intending to release a double album, but later chose to release just a single LP with six tracks: 'Young Man Blues', 'Substitute', 'Summertime Blues', Shakin' All Over', 'My Generation' and 'Magic Bus'.

Geoffrey Anketell Studdert Kennedy, MC (1883–1929), aka 'Woodbine Willie'

Kennedy was an English-Anglican priest and poet. He is best remembered by his nickname 'Woodbine Willie', earned during the war for lavishing Woodbine cigarettes along with spiritual aid on injured and dying soldiers with no regard for his own safety.

He was born in Leeds, the seventh of nine children born to Jeanette Anketell and William Studdert Kennedy, vicar of St Mary's, in the impoverished Quarry Hill area. Studdert Kennedy was educated at Leeds Grammar School and Trinity College, Dublin, where he graduated in Classics and Divinity in 1904. He then trained at Ripon Clergy College before going on to posts in Rugby and Worcester.

Woodbine Willie, 1918.

Apparently, his charismatic, unorthodox way converted more men over a pint of beer than most vicars could achieve in their churches in a lifetime. At the outbreak of war Studdert Kennedy volunteered as a chaplain to the army on the Western Front. In 1917 he was awarded the Military Cross at Messines Ridge in Flanders after he dashed into no man's land to fetch morphine and tend the wounded during an attack on the German frontline. His citation read: 'For conspicuous gallantry and devotion to duty. He showed the greatest courage and disregard for his own safety in attending to the wounded under heavy fire. He searched shell holes for our own and enemy wounded, assisting them to the dressing station, and his cheerfulness and endurance had a splendid effect upon all ranks in the front line trenches, which he constantly visited' (*The London Gazette*, 14 August 1917).

A published poet, he authored *Rough Rhymes of a Padre* (1918) and *More Rough Rhymes* (1919). During the First World War he was an enthusiastic promoter of the British war machine. Attached to a bayonet-training unit, he toured with boxers and wrestlers to give morale-boosting speeches and demonstrations about the usefulness and efficacy of the bayonet. However, his Damascene moment came when he stopped talking and started listening to the soldiers, spreading their views on ending the war, their distaste for the monarchy, and their hopes for the end of poverty back home. His poems, many of which are written in working-class Yorkshire dialect, project their views in their own words and language. Nevertheless, he apparently believed that in principle it was better for young men to be challenged by facing German guns than by resorting to prostitutes and so established self-help groups for men tempted by prostitutes and drink.

When he died (in Liverpool, on a speaking tour) in 1929 at the age of forty-five 2,000 people flocked to his funeral in Worcester, lining the roads from Worcester Cathedral to his old parish church of St Paul's. In a marvellous and apt gesture, they tossed packets of Woodbines onto the passing cortege. The plaque inside the cathedral proclaims him as 'A Poet: A Prophet: A Passionate seeker after Truth'.

Xmas Cracker

Better known, and badged, as 'Christmas Cracker', this was a Yuletide brew launched by Tetley's. This is how the brewery described it:

> Tetley's Christmas Cracker is brewed to get you in the mood for Yule. Dark and Contemplative, Christmas Cracker's wintery warmth delivers a complex, rich and satisfying 4.3% ale for the festive season. A subtle suggestion of vanilla and a delicate hop aroma combine to make sure this is one 'Cracker' you'll want to see pulled again and again!

On 5 November 2008, Carlsberg UK announced their plans to close the plant in 2011, moving production to Northampton. The company was criticised for slyly choosing to announce the closure the day after Barack Obama was elected US president to ensure the news would not get any significant coverage in the British national press. In 2010, production of Tetley's cask products was transferred to Banks's brewery in Wolverhampton. Tetley Smoothflow was brewed by Coors in Tadcaster and Tetley keg Dark Mild, Mild and Imperial by Cameron's of Hartlepool. The final Leeds brew was on 22 February 2011. Lager production was transferred to Northampton.

Pulling the Tetley's Xmas cracker.

RAF Yeadon & the Avro Shadow Factory

The aerodrome, now Leeds Bradford Airport, opened as the Leeds and Bradford Municipal Aerodrome, Yeadon Aerodrome, on 17 October 1931 and was operated by the Yorkshire Aeroplane Club for Leeds and Bradford corporations. Scheduled flights began in 1935 with a service by North Eastern Airways from Heston Aerodrome in London to Cramlington at Newcastle-upon-Tyne, later extended to Edinburgh's Turnhouse. Civil aviation was, of course, suspended in 1939.

In 1942 Avro built a new factory to produce military aircraft just to the north of the aerodrome. Around 5,515 aircraft were produced and delivered from Yeadon during the war including Ansons (over 4,500), Bristol Blenheims (250), Lancasters (695), Yorks (45) and Lincolns (25).

Two new runways, taxiways and extra hangars made Yeadon an important site for military aircraft test-flying. The Avro factory was camouflaged, replicating the original field pattern, apparently carried out by people from the film industry, and had dummy cows placed on the roof of the factory to fool German airmen into thinking that it was just a field of cattle beneath them. There were also imitation farm buildings, stone walls and a duck pond placed around the factory. Hedges and bushes made out of fabric were periodically changed to match the changing colours of the seasons. Dummy animals were moved around daily to mimic activity. It all obviously worked because enemy bombers never detected the factory.

At its height during the war there was a staff of more than 17,500 people employed at Avro Yeadon. It was one of twenty-six 'shadow factories' and also the largest in Europe with a site of around 34 acres. The factory operated round the clock with workers on shift sixty-nine hours a week on a three-day followed by a three-night basis. Many of the workers were female, local girls supplemented by large numbers bussed in from all over West Yorkshire. The Ministry of Aircraft Production (MAP) built temporary homes or provided accommodation, for example, on the Westfield Estate in Yeadon and Greenbanks at Horsforth, for workers who lived at a distance from the Avro assembly plant.

British shadow factories came about from the government Shadow Scheme of 1935 in an attempt to meet the urgent need for aircraft using technology from the motor industry. The term 'shadow' has nothing to do with obscurity or secrecy, but describes the skilled motor industry staff shadowing their own motor industry operations.

Z

Zeppelins

Leeds was never bombed by a Zeppelin, but, naturally, precautions were put in place in and around the city. Special constables were tasked with keeping watch, mainly from the roof of the Town Hall, and with raising the alarm. Spotting a Zeppelin would trigger a reduction in gas and electricity supply, a dimming of all lights and stopping the trams. The only two raids to speak of were in September and November 1916 when Zeppelins passed over Collingham and Pontefract Park: incendiaries were dropped on the grounds of Harewood House when the Germans perhaps confused the Aire with the Wharfe. The *Daily News* offered free insurance against Zeppelin damage!

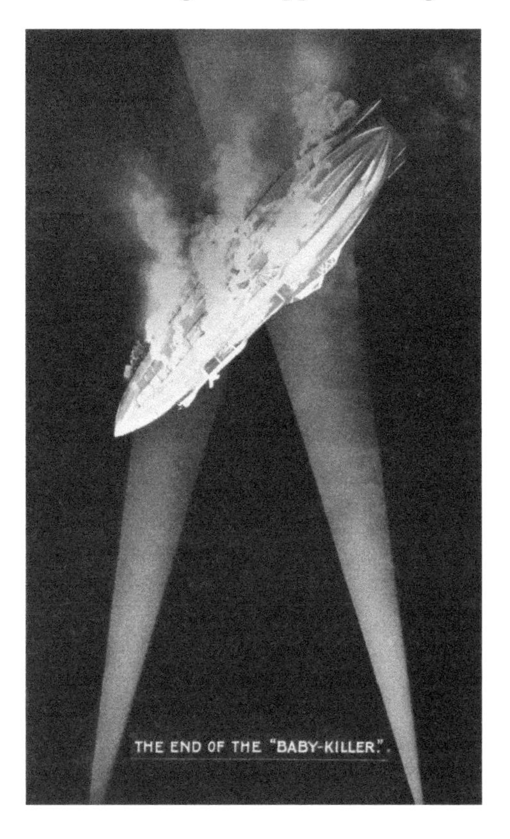

A British propoganda postcard. The text reads: 'The End of the "Baby-Killer"'. It depicts the demise of Schütte-Lanz SL 11 over Cuffley, who was shot down by Lieutenant Leefe-Robinson on 3 September 1916; he was awarded the VC for this action.

About the Author

Paul Chrystal has Classics degrees from the universities of Hull and Southampton. After gaining these he went into medical publishing for forty or so years but now combines this with writing features for national newspapers and history magazines, as well as appearing regularly on BBC local radio, on the BBC World Service and Radio 4's PM programme. In 2018 Paul contributed to a six-part series for BBC2 'celebrating the history of some of Britain's most iconic craft industries' – in this case chocolate in York. He has been history advisor for a number of York tourist attractions and is the author of 100 or so books on a wide range of subjects, including many on Yorkshire. He is a regular reviewer for and contributor to *Classics for All*. From 2019 he is editor of *York Historian*, the journal of the Yorkshire Architectural and York Archaeological Society. Also in 2019, Paul is guest speaker for the prestigious Vassar College New York's London Programme in association with Goldsmith University. Paul lives near York.

paul.chrystal@btinternet.com

Also by Paul Chrystal

Central Leeds Central Through Time, Leeds's Military Legacy, Leeds in 50 Buildings, Historic England: Leeds, Old Bramley, Whitby at Work, Bradford at Work, The Confectionery Industry in Yorkshire, Old Saltaire & Shipley, Pubs in and Around the Yorkshire Dales, Old Skipton, Old Sheffield, Doncaster at Work, Tadcaster Through Time, Selby & Goole Through Time, The Vale of York Through Time, The Pubs of Harrogate & Knaresborough, Secret Harrogate, Harrogate Through Time, The North York Moors Through Time, Secret Knaresborough, Knaresborough Through Time, Huddersfield Through Time and *Changing Scarborough.*